Documentary Monographs
in Modern Art
general editor: Paul Cummings

DAVID SMITH

edited by
Garnett McCoy

Allen Lane

Frontispiece: David Smith on *Cubi III*. Photograph by Dan Budnick, 1962.

First published in the United States of America in 1973
by Praeger Publishers, Inc., New York

First published in Great Britain in 1973

Allen Lane
A Division of Penguin Books Ltd
21 John Street, London WC1N 2BT

ISBN 0 7139 0424 0

Printed in the United States of America

contents

III INTERVIEWS

IV LETTERS

V WRITING AND CRITICISM ABOUT DAVID SMITH

list of illustrations

(Unless otherwise noted in the captions, all illustrations are part of the David Smith Papers in the Archives of American Art, Smithsonian Institution, Washington, D.C.)

TEXT ILLUSTRATIONS

preface

A book of David Smith's speeches, articles, and other writings is an exercise in paradox. Smith never regarded himself as an accomplished writer or speaker, and he found both activities onerous. They took time away from his sculpture. "I'm not a good writer," he wrote to Jean Xceron after finishing his article on Julio González, "but I did as good as I could and I have no apologies. But I could have made two sculptures while I worked on it." And to Robert Laurent he said, "We all talk too much about art and don't do enough of it. I'm withdrawing from the talk from now on." He also felt that he alienated people with the bluntness of his remarks, and in February, 1954, wrote that "this speech writing is so difficult (and useless) that I'm going to draw in."

Moreover, he felt, and often expressed, a profound distrust of the written word. Verbal communication was to him an untrustworthy element, inferior to visual impression, susceptible to manipulation and confusion. "Tradition comes wrapped in word pictures," he remarked to an audience in 1952. "Words are the traps which lead the nonartists into cliché thinking and conclusive evaluation. . . . We must revolt against all word authority. Our only language is vision."

Yet he contradicted this belief on a grand scale. While it is true that he wrote few articles specifically for publication, he lectured frequently in the early 1950's at meetings of other artists, to students, and to groups of art lovers. Far from their being spontaneous discourses, these speeches were usually carefully worked from notes and consciously developed through a series of drafts. Smith was, in fact, quite deliberate in the expression of his views. Some of the lectures were reworkings of earlier ones. As he wrote to Henry Hope in 1953, "I sing one song of mostly personal views and my own work procedures. There is the same subject in most of my papers."

The effect of his song is a clear statement of several ideas he felt strongly about—the iniquity of verbalism, the identity of the artist, the dead hand of tradition. Together with frequent autobiographical references, comments on technique, and advice to students, these themes reflect Smith's profound concern with his work and his efforts to define the nature of the artist. The two interviews and the letters published here extend these preoccupations in a more personal and direct manner.

Most of the documents in this book are among the large collection of David Smith Papers at the Archives of American Art, Smithsonian Institution. No serious research or writing on David Smith can be conducted without reference to these papers, whose variety and detail make them one of the Archives's richest groups of an artist's personal records. They are described at some length in my "The David Smith Papers," *Archives of American Art Journal,* April, 1968.

My grateful thanks are here extended to Ira Lowe, Clement Greenberg, and Robert Motherwell, executors of the David Smith Estate, for their permission to publish material from these records. I also want to express my particular appreciation to Lucille Corcos and Edgar Levy for permission to quote from David Smith's letters to them. Additional letters to Marian Willard and Robert Nunnelley are also published with their kind permission.

I am separately indebted to Clement Greenberg for permission to reprint his article on Smith in the Institute of Contemporary Art, University of Pennsylvania catalogue of a David Smith exhibition held in February and March, 1964.

I am also obliged to the publications *Architectural Record, Art International, Art News, Arts and Architecture, Living Arts,* and *The Nation* for articles by and on David Smith published in their respective pages.

Many photographs of the works of art reproduced here were taken by David Smith himself. These appear with the permission of their owners, who are individually acknowledged with each illustration.

Finally I want to thank Miss Mary Farrell, Miss Ellyn Childs, and Mr. Paul Cummings for their indispensable help in the organization and editing of this book.

Garnett McCoy
October, 1972

introduction, chronology

Introduction

"Art isn't made for the wealthy," David Smith once wrote. "It comes from the life of the artist—out of his own life, his own environment." An understanding of David Smith's work, then, must begin with a knowledge of his character as it took shape and grew under the influences of early childhood, of school and factory, of friends and associates, of success and fulfillment. That character, contradictory in so many ways, is not an easy one to grasp. One can only speculate on the source of the furies that drove him. But one can, by a study of the man, reach some awareness of his nature and in so doing achieve a deeper perception of his art. For description of art itself, he believed, "results in verbal sterility. Describing the life from which it sprang is its history."

He was born on March 9, 1906, in Decatur, Indiana, a small town his great-grandfather had helped to found in the northeastern part of the state. His father was a telephone company official and, in an old American tradition, an intermittent and unsuccessful inventor. His mother seems to have been the stronger parent and was certainly the stronger influence on his development. A teacher and a firm Methodist, she lived within a framework of traditional puritan virtues—piety, hard work, thrift, unquestioning acceptance of conventional proprieties. She hoped that her son would become a teacher, too. She evidently had great determination and resilience, and while her son soon rejected her middle-class values, he absorbed from her a profound belief in work and a stern sense of discipline. He was never a bohemian. And if he later railed against his mother's penurious ways and the provincialism of midwestern small-town life, he was always acutely conscious of money and security or, as he called it, survival.

Smith's most conspicuous trait was a furious, passionate, even violent energy. His capacity for sustained hard physical labor was astonishing. Eventually this energy found its outlet in the forms and intractable materials he chose to work with. But it remained a mixed blessing and occasionally, under the pressure of rage and frustration, operated destructively against himself and those around him.

From his earliest childhood, Smith displayed a fierce craving for independence. He regarded his grandmother's house as a refuge from what he felt was parental oppression and sometimes ran off to stay with her. In an often recalled incident, the three- or four-year-old David, tied to a tree to prevent his leaving the yard, modeled a lion from the surrounding mud. This exhibition of precocious talent brought extravagant praise from his mother. But apparently it was an isolated effort, although the pictures in his grandmother's Bible and in other books made a deep impression on him. Unlike the recollections of many other artists, Smith's contain no references to childhood painting and drawing activities pursued with single-minded devotion.

In 1921, the family moved to nearby Paulding, Ohio, where Smith went to high school. His boyhood seems to have been an ordinary one of chores, pranks, daredevil escapades, and fascination with mechanical objects, especially railroad trains. He would jump back and forth from one moving freight train to another on a parallel track. He exploded dynamite charges in the fields. In one memorable episode, he primed and set off the Civil War cannon in the town square. He worked resentfully at jobs on Saturdays and in the summers in beet fields and in stores to make money for his education.

In addition to the usual high school courses, he took two years of mechanical drawing. He also subscribed to a correspondence course in drawing, the first indication of a serious interest in art. He gained a local reputation as a cartoonist and served as artist for his high school yearbook.

In September, 1924, Smith went to Ohio University in Athens, where he spent an unsatisfactory year. His grades, even in mechanical drawing, were poor except for a B plus and an A in art structure and a B minus in freehand drawing. By this time he had definite ambitions for an art career, and he bitterly resented the inadequacy of his college art teaching, which was chiefly concerned with art education.

At the end of the school year he went to South Bend, Indiana, and worked for the summer at the Studebaker plant. Years later, this experience took on an almost legendary quality. It gave him, he felt, a feeling for industrial forms, training in the handling of tools and factory equipment, and a sense of identification with working men. "I know workmen, their vision," he later wrote, "because between college years I have worked on Studebaker's production line." In 1932, when he discovered the possibilities of welded iron and steel for the making of sculpture, he recalled the weeks at Studebaker and felt that they had prepared him for just that form of aesthetic expression. While some of this was no doubt romanticized recall, the months spent at the factory made a lasting impression.

At the end of the summer Smith enrolled at Notre Dame, but left it almost immediately. He worked briefly for Studebaker's finance department, sold bonds, and moved to Washington, D.C., to a job with the Morris Plan Bank, a cooperative banking arrangement popular at the time. In Washington he attended college for the last time, taking a course in poetry at George Washington University. In the summer of 1926, the Morris Plan Bank transferred him to its New York office.

Since high school, his goal had been to study art, preferably in New

York. He arrived there filled with artistic aspirations but without knowing how to proceed. It was his singular good fortune shortly after his arrival to meet Dorothy Dehner, an art student from California who lived at the same rooming house. When Miss Dehner told him about the Art Students League he enrolled the next day. Acting on her advice, he began his studies under Richard Lahey and John Sloan.

Smith was tall and very thin, attractive, enthusiastic, and impressionable. He had a compelling charm and enormous self-confidence. He enjoyed an active social life and continued to work at his job, later doing freelance art work that included assignments for A. G. Spalding and N. W. Ayer and Sons. For a short period he drove a cab. In December, 1927, he and Dorothy Dehner were married.

Smith studied off and on at the League for five years. In addition to Lahey and Sloan, he worked with Kimon Nicolaides and, of greater importance to his development, Jan Matulka, who had studied under Hans Hofmann and who encouraged an interest in Cubism. He later wrote that he got from Sloan a "feeling of knowing the artist's position as a rebel or as one in revolt against the status quo," and from Nicolaides a "feeling for sensitivity in a line." But "Matulka was a guy I'd rather give more credit than anyone else."

Another significant influence on the Smiths at the League was Thomas Furlong and his wife, Weber, secretary of the League. The Furlongs were more aware of the current trends in European art than most of the League circle, and even before Smith had encountered Matulka, they implanted in him a sympathetic feeling for abstract art. The Furlongs invited the young couple to stay as paying guests at their summer place near Bolton Landing, a resort village on the west shore of Lake George. In the summer of 1929, the Smiths bought a place nearby—Fox Farm on Tick Ridge Road, about three miles from Bolton Landing. It had an old frame house, a barn, a woodshed, and a good stand of timber.

The Furlongs also introduced the Smiths to John Graham, a man who was to have a profound influence on Smith in the 1930's. By his own account a White Russian cavalry officer in the Revolution, Graham fled to New York, studied painting, and became a highly sophisticated connoisseur and authority on primitive and modern art. He had a brilliant and serious mind and a flamboyant character, and he made a point of keeping up with the younger advanced artists in New York. As adviser to and buyer for collectors of African sculpture, especially Frank Crowninshield, editor of *Vanity Fair,* he moved between Paris and New York and brought to his protégés in America news of the latest developments in French painting and sculpture.

The Smiths often visited Graham's house and listened to his accounts of Picasso and the Spanish sculptor Julio González. Smith would sit poring over the art magazines Graham kept, among them the French *Cahiers d'Art,* and it was there that he came across the illustrated article on González's welded sculpture that awakened him to the possibilities of working with iron and steel—materials he had already handled in an industrial setting.

Graham introduced the Smiths to other abstract artists working in New York—men like Arshile Gorky, Stuart Davis, Milton Avery, and Jean Xceron. Having shifted his ideological views from an earlier anti-revolutionary position to a championing of the left, Graham exerted a strong political influence. Later he would abandon both Picasso and the left, but in the 1930's he was politically, as well as artistically, radical and on at least one occasion took the Smiths to an open meeting of the John Reed Club, the left-wing artists group. By 1935, like most of his generation in the arts, Smith was a staunch supporter of radical causes.

In 1931, inspired by romantic visions of Gauguin in Tahiti, the Smiths left New York for St. Thomas in the Virgin Islands. There they painted, and there Smith made his first tentative experiments in sculpture. By making indentations in and slightly carving small pieces of coral found on the beach he created abstract objects suggesting figures. Although he continued to concentrate on painting, he experimented with sculpture again on his return to New York in the summer of 1932 by fashioning constructions from bits of wood and metal, in some cases attaching them to canvas. He also began working with a forge in his woodshed studio at Bolton Landing.

After reading about González's work and discussing it with Graham, Smith bought welding equipment, which he attempted to use in a back room of his apartment in Brooklyn. The space was cramped and things often caught on fire. The landlord complained. One day that winter, as he and Dorothy were out walking, they saw on the ferry dock at the end of Atlantic Avenue "a long rambly junky looking shack called Terminal Iron Works." She suggested he work there instead of at home. "Next morning I walked in," he wrote later, "and was met by a big Irishman named Blackburn. 'I'm an artist; I have a welding outfit. I'd like to work here.' 'Hell yes, move in.' "

Smith's years at the Terminal Iron Works with Blackburn and his associate Buckhorn were probably the happiest of his life. "I learned a lot from those guys," he wrote in the late 1940's, "and from the machinist that worked for them named Robert Henry. Played chess with him, learned a lot about lathe work from him. . . . I met about everyone on the waterfront in our area. Many who were very good friends provided me with metal. Kind of a nice fraternity down there. Enjoyed this. Those guys were fine—never made fun of my work—took it as a matter of course." He never forgot those years, As late as the 1960's he wrote in

David Smith

a notebook, "Once in a lifetime you meet an iron works. . . . Once in a lifetime you meet two Irishmen named Blackburn and Buckhorn to whom you present yourself with one set of equipment and practically no money and no WPA yet and they say OK move in and it runs—and you are in—not only there but on the whole waterfront." After Smith became famous enough to be written up in *Life,* an old drinking companion, Hugh Brady, wrote to him recalling "nostalgic memories of our association close to 'Red Mike's Saloon' where we had the pleasure of many philosophical and political discussions."

In spite of his welding equipment and his shop at the Terminal Iron Works, Smith continued to alternate between painting and sculpture, and it was not until 1935 that he definitely committed himself to the latter medium. As he states in a 1956 letter to Jean Xceron, "Remember May, 1935, when we walked down Fifty-seventh Street after your show . . . how you influenced me to concentrate on sculpture. I'm of course forever glad that you did, it's more my energy, though I make two hundred color drawings a year and sometimes painting. . . . But I paint or draw as a sculptor, I have no split identity as I did in 1935."

In the fall of 1935, the Smiths left for an extended trip to Europe. They were met in Paris by John Graham, who guided them to artists, museums, and private collections. In December they moved on to Athens, where they painted, studied ancient Greek art, and investigated archaeological sites. In the spring they returned to Paris briefly, stopped in London, and then embarked on a four-week visit to the Soviet Union. They returned to the United States in July, 1936.

The tour was an important educational experience. Smith had found it difficult to work while abroad, but he learned much from his studies of museum and private collections of African and ancient Greek sculpture and European Renaissance painting. Both his commitment to sculpture and his ideological convictions were strengthened by what he saw.

During the 1930's, the Smiths spent most of the summers and falls at Bolton Landing and winters in a succession of apartments in Brooklyn. For much of the period they derived a small but steady income from the New Deal art programs, first the Treasury Relief Art Project, on which Smith served as a technical supervisor for the mural division, and later the WPA's Federal Art Project, under which he produced sculpture. In later years he often expressed approval of the Federal Art Project as an important factor in the advancement of American art because it enabled artists to pursue their own work.

Problems of job security and working conditions under the Project, together with the general political agitation aroused by the Depression, led to the formation of a vigorous artists union. An active member, Smith participated in meetings, street demonstrations, and discussions.

His first recorded speech, a strong defense of abstract art at a time when that means of expression suffered from hostility or indifference, was given at a symposium on abstract art sponsored by the union, and the union printed excerpts from it in its journal.

"The great majority of abstract artists," he wrote about 1940, "are anti-fascist and socially conscious." This theme of social consciousness often appears in his notes of the 1930's and 1940's, and vestiges of it recur in later years as well. He struggled, unsuccessfully in the end, to reconcile the apparent contradiction between his ideological beliefs and his dedication to abstract art. Since the latter had no explicit revolutionary and emotional content and failed in any case to win working-class appreciation, it was regarded by many radical artists as a frivolous exercise in formalism. Smith felt that the problem lay not with abstract art itself, which he saw as the true revolutionary art, but with the visual corruption created in the people by commercial exploitation of visual images. He also denied the validity of the then-accepted social protest art favored by conventional social realist painters. "They [i.e., the social realist painters] do not want unpleasant revision," he wrote in the late 1930's, "any more than they want to be mentally disturbed by abstraction. Social comment is not the art of the people."

But if abstract art was the art of the people, the people failed to realize it. In later years Smith's views on art bore a distinct elitist tinge, but his commitment to the labor movement remained strong in the forties. In a note written in 1948, he claims that "by choice I identify myself with working men and still belong to Local 2054 United Steelworkers of America. I belong by craft—yet the subject of aesthetics introduces a breach. I suppose it is because I believe in the future, [in] a working man's society, and in that society I hope to find a place. In this society I find little place for identify[ing] myself economically."

Although some of Smith's standing sculpture of the late 1930's and 1940's reflects a powerful if indirect social comment, his most explicit statements of protest are in the fifteen Medals for Dishonor, completed in 1940. Several things he saw in Europe contributed to the concept of this group—Sumerian seals, a series of German war medals, the paintings of Bosch and Breughel. In a travel notebook he refers to "combined surrealist symbolism of king's men cutting people in two. . . . Whipping—tortures of royalty on people—hanging—stretching—choking with hot water—chopping off hands—recording . . . with sanctimonious faces henchmen of wealth." These influences, together with an interest in the intaglio process, a feeling for surrealism, and a desire to express his political beliefs, led to a prolonged experimentation conducted at night between 1937 and 1939. After several unsatisfactory attempts at

David Smith

casting at the Terminal Iron Works, he had the medallions cast in bronze by a jeweler.

An exhibition of the medallions at the Willard Gallery was arranged, and Smith asked the novelist William Blake, whose *The Painter and the Lady* he had recently read and admired, to write an introduction to the catalogue. "The medallions," he wrote to Blake, "depict the horrors of war, its causes, those who inspire and lead it, its resulting destruction. These medals are dedicated [to] the perpetrators." Blake and his wife, Christina Stead, also a novelist, were so impressed by the series they each wrote an introduction. Smith himself composed statements to accompany each of the medals. Shown in November, 1940, the exhibition received favorable critical notice and some publicity, but no sales.

For Smith, the 1930's were essentially a period of intensive experimentation in a variety of sculptural styles derived especially from Cubism and Constructivism. He early displayed a grasp of sculptural form, exploiting it both in massive arrangements of planes and solids and in intricately worked constructions, often with clear associative patterns delineating animal and human features and landscape and interior settings. In some instances he incorporated tools and other utilitarian objects in the work. From the very first welded pieces, and earlier in wood and metal constructions, his sculpture was firmly in the abstract idiom. Much of this early work shows his indebtedness to the European innovators in welded sculpture—Picasso, González, and Gargallo.

According to Smith's later recollection he had shown paintings and drawings at the ACA Gallery as early as 1932 and later at the Ferargil Galleries. He also remembered his first welded heads being shown at the Julian Levy Gallery in 1934. His first one-man show took place at Marian Willard's East River Gallery early in 1938, beginning an association which would last until the mid-1950's. During the early 1940's, Smith was represented in a number of exhibitions in various parts of the country and held a second one-man show at the Neumann-Willard Gallery in March, 1940. This, together with the Medals for Dishonor exhibition later that year, gave him prominence in the New York art world. There were few sales.

The year 1940 was in many ways a turning point in Smith's life, marking as it did his permanent move away from New York, the end of his connection with the Federal Art Project and its related political activities, and the beginning of critical recognition. While Smith had been closely associated both socially and professionally with a circle of artists living in Brooklyn and Manhattan—Graham, Edgar and Lucille Corcos Levy, Stuart Davis, Willem de Kooning, Mischa Resnikoff—he now chose the isolation of Bolton Landing and the financial hazards of unemployment. With intervals of teaching and occasional visits to the city, he clung to this position for the rest of his life. It suited his passionate desire for independence, but it also created sometimes intolerable strains in his personal life and led to an often embittered loneliness.

At first, since there was an immediate need for an income, Smith worked as a machinist in Glens Falls, New York. In 1942, with war production in full swing, he and Dorothy moved to Schenectady where he found a job as a welder at the American Locomotive Company plant producing locomotives and tanks. His schedule was demanding. "When I was through work at the factory at 8 A.M.," he later recalled, "I would drive two or three days a week, forty miles to Saratoga to the monument works of Mallory and La Brake where I carved marble for six hours. Drove back to Schenectady and got to bed—got up at 11:30 for the midnight shift. . . . About once a week I would get my sleep over in the day, and we would drive to Saratoga for a night session—get a model to pose in a friend's studio—just to keep drawing and to maintain my identity as an artist."

There was little time for sculpture, and during the two years spent in Schenectady Smith completed only a few pieces. But the experience was a valuable one, technically and also for the sense of scale he developed. Working on locomotives and tanks was deeply satisfying as a physical and psychological commitment, and Smith looked forward to applying what he learned to larger works of art than he had been used to making.

In 1944, during one of the periodic layoffs from the factory, the Smiths returned to Bolton Landing. They had saved some money, and with the proceeds from the sale of timber on the farm, they finished a new studio and designed a house to replace the old frame structure they had lived in. This new house, built with little outside help, was a plain cinder-block dwelling overlooking a pasture and with a glimpse of Lake George between two hills in the distance. It was finished in 1948.

In 1947–48, Smith began two activities that he pursued sporadically throughout the following decade—teaching and lecturing. While he undertook both pursuits for the money they brought, he regarded them with great seriousness and achieved a reputation as an outspoken and direct advocate and a dedicated teacher. He also relieved his financial pressures by obtaining Guggenheim fellowships in both 1950 and 1951, an indication of the mounting esteem he claimed. This initial postwar period ended in 1950 when Smith and Dorothy Dehner were separated. It was the end of an epoch and of a way of life.

Following his return to Bolton Landing in 1944 and continuing through the Guggenheim-grants period, Smith worked his way through one of his most prolific and inventive periods. His sculpture of this time

David Smith

shows an evolution away from the smaller-scale pieces of the 1930's and toward an intensely felt and sometimes highly elaborated private symbolism. Two typical examples of this latter tendency are *Home of the Welder*, 1945, and *The Cathedral*, 1950. In the former, a complex interior setting holds various representations of figures and objects—a woman's body, a dog's head, a millstone and chain, a phallic welding torch, a flowering plant. In *The Cathedral*, one of the last of the personal statement pieces, Smith presents an open structure designed to suggest a church with a symbolic claw, a prostrate man, a coin. In one of his few accounts of the meaning of a work, he pointed out that *The Cathedral* held a "symbol of power—the state, the church or any individual's private mansion built at the expense of others."

Some of these pieces have been interpreted as Smith's effort to transform into visual metaphor the psychic pressures he felt. Although he ceased working in this style in the early 1950's, the pressures remained, a fact made poignantly clear in a long passage from a notebook of the period.

The heights come seldom—the steadiness is always chewing the gut—seldom without a raw spot—the times of true height are so rare, some seemingly high spots being suspected later as illusion. . . . the future—the factory or the classroom, both undesirable yet possible at present, but in twenty years neither will be open . . . and nothing has been as great or as wonderful as I envisioned. I have confidence in my ability to create beyond what I've done, and always at the time beyond what I do. . . . It would be nice to not be so lonesome sometimes—months pass without even the acquaintance of a mind, acquaintances are pure waste—why do I measure my life by works—the other time seems waste—Can the life measured by work be illusion?—yet this standard seems farthest from illusion of any measure—and the way it stands much is lacking—and a certain body time tells that it can't be had, if it didn't come by now and so much work to be done—it comes too fast to get it down in solids—too little time, too little money. Why can't it stay as vision—for who else do I make it? . . . If I walk fifteen miles through mountains I'm exhausted enough to want to rest, and the mind won't—enjoying nature is only occasional and not complete enough—but more so than artificial stimulations of jazz and bop and beer which race along without the mind and leave me feeling cheated—I hate to go to bed—to stay alive longer—I've slipped up on time—it all didn't get in—the warpage is in me.

In 1953, while teaching at the University of Arkansas, Smith married Jean Freas of Washington, D.C. Their two daughters, Rebecca and Candida, were born in 1954 and 1955. A few years later this second marriage also broke up, and thereafter Smith lived alone on his hillside with occasional visits from friends. His daughters visited him, too. Smith felt a deep emotional involvement with them that he expressed in letters and in his dedication to them of a number of late sculptures.

There were other changes in the old pattern of his life. A growing estrangement took place between Smith and some of his friends of the 1930's. He built a new circle of intimates—Herman Cherry, Clement Greenberg, Helen Frankenthaler, Robert Motherwell, and Kenneth Noland. In 1956, he parted company with Marian Willard, his dealer of nearly twenty years.

In the art world he had, by the mid-1950's, a reputation as one of the most important sculptors in America, and, with the triumph of postwar American art and the rapid expansion of the market, his work was for the first time in demand. The official accolade was bestowed in 1957 when the Museum of Modern Art held a retrospective exhibition of his work. Yet, with increasing critical and economic success, a strain of arrogance and harshness became more pronounced in his statements and letters.

His work of these years is characterized by a growing monumentality of scale and form and by greater simplicity and formal plastic inventiveness. Figurative elements remained in Smith's work to the end, but in the fifties and sixties there are more nonobjective juxtapositions of planes and cursive forms, culminating in the enormous and formidable Cubi, Zig, and Wagon series produced toward the end of the sculptor's life.

In 1962, Smith accepted an invitation to spend a month at Voltri, near Genoa in Italy. The contents of an abandoned factory and several workmen were made available to him by the Italian Government. The burst of creativity evoked by this circumstance brought forth twenty-six sculptures in thirty days and later resulted in additional pieces made from metal and tools Smith brought back with him to Bolton Landing.

The culminating achievement of Smith's career as a sculptor was the Cubi series, begun in 1961 and continued until his death four years later. These huge sculptures, some of them more than ten feet high and weighing over a ton, incorporated massive cubes and cylinders of burnished stainless steel. In their expansiveness and stylistic organization, they represent a final working out of formal problems encountered as early as the 1930's, as well as a probing exploration of new sculptural possibilities.

By 1965, if Smith's name was not as well known to the general public as Calder's or Pollock's, it was not for lack of exposure. He had been the subject of many articles in art journals, popular magazines, catalogue introductions, and interviews on radio and television. He had been represented in innumerable exhibitions at home and abroad, and the price he could command for his work was high. His old scorn of collectors was softened somewhat under the influence of success. His creativity was undiminished.

In February, 1965, President Johnson appointed Smith to the National Council on the Arts, and on May 21, two days before he died, he had notice that he would be receiving an invitation "to attend the first White House Festival of the Arts." Respectability was at hand; the rage so bitterly expressed in the Medals for Dishonor seemed dormant.

On May 23, Smith drove his pickup truck to Bennington, Vermont, where he was scheduled to give a lecture in the evening. He attended a party at a house in the country, and on the way to the college his truck ran off the road and capsized. He died that night from a fractured skull. Only a few days before, a youthful admirer had written him, quoting prophetic lines from Dante:

> I had not known that death
> Had undone so many.

Chronology

1906   David Roland Smith born March 9 in Decatur, Indiana, a small town in the northeastern corner of the state where his father was a telephone technician and his mother had been a teacher.

1921   Smith family moves to Paulding, Ohio, another small town not far from Decatur. In high school, David Smith achieves reputation as a cartoonist and serves as artist for the school yearbook. Subscribes to a correspondence course in drawing from the Cleveland Art School.

1924   Graduates from high school and enters Ohio University in Athens, Ohio.

1925   After two semesters, leaves Ohio University and spends the summer as an assembly-line worker in the Studebaker plant in South Bend, Indiana. In the fall, enters Notre Dame University in South Bend, but leaves almost immediately. Sells bonds. Moves to Washington, D.C., to work for the Morris Plan Bank.

1926   Takes poetry course at George Washington University. Moves to New York in the summer to work for the Acceptance Corporation, a branch of the Morris Plan Bank. Lives in a rooming house near Columbia University, where he meets Dorothy

Dehner, a student at the Art Students League. She persuades him to study there under Richard Lahey.

1927   Continues evening courses at Art Students League under Lahey and John Sloan. Smith and Dorothy Dehner are married December 24.

1928   Takes various jobs and studies under Jan Matulka and others. In the spring and summer, visits Dorothy Dehner's family in California. Becomes friendly with Thomas and Weber Furlong, who introduce the Smiths to Bolton Landing on Lake George.

1929   Continues studies with Matulka and Kimon Nicolaides. The Smiths buy Fox Farm near Bolton Landing. Through the Furlongs they meet John Graham, painter and theorist.

1931   Inspired by romantic visions of the tropics, the Smiths spend several months on St. Thomas in the Virgin Islands. There he creates first sculptural constructions with found pieces of coral.

1932   Return to New York in June. Continues experiments with sculptural objects, sometimes attaching them to canvas, but chief interest is still painting. Begins work with forge at Bolton Landing. Sees reproductions of welded sculpture by Picasso and Julio González in *Cahiers d'Art*.

1933   First welded piece, one of Head series. In late 1933 or early 1934, Smith finds Terminal Iron Works, a machinist shop on the Brooklyn waterfront. He establishes his studio there.

1934   Takes position as technical supervisor of mural painting in Treasury Relief Art Project, a New Deal art program.

1935   Commits himself to sculpture as his artistic medium, although he continues to paint and draw, too. In the fall, the Smiths go to Europe, where they visit museums and private collections in France. In December, they move on to Athens.

1936   Work and study in Athens followed by visits to Paris, London, and the Soviet Union. Return to New York in July.

1937   Joins Federal Art Project, the WPA art program, for which he makes sculpture. Begins work on Medals for Dishonor series of medallions attacking war and other social evils.

1938   In January, Smith's first one-man show of sculpture and drawings held at Marian Willard's East River Gallery in New York.

1939   Smith's sculpture represented in several group exhibitions in New York, Minneapolis, and at Skidmore College in Saratoga Springs. Writes article for an unpublished work, *Art for the Mil-*

lions, sponsored by the Federal Art Project. Continues work on Medals for Dishonor.

1940   Second one-man show held at Neumann-Willard Gallery in March. First recorded speech given at symposium on abstract art held by the artists union, the United American Artists. In the summer the Smiths move permanently to Bolton Landing, where their house and studio are thereafter called Terminal Iron Works. Work completed on the Medals for Dishonor, which were shown at the Willard Gallery in November. This and the March exhibition reviewed at length in the *Springfield Republican* by Elizabeth McCausland.

1941   One-man shows held at Minneapolis, St. Paul, and Kalamazoo. Smith works as a machinist at Glens Falls, New York. Begins building and equipping a studio-workshop on his Bolton Landing property.

1942   Takes wartime welding job at the American Locomotive Company plant in Schenectady. One-man show at Walker Art Center in Minneapolis.

1943   Smith's *Interior,* shown in a group exhibition at the Willard and Buchholz galleries in January, receives highly favorable notice from Clement Greenberg in *The Nation.* One-man show held at Willard Gallery in April. Designs series of medals for the Chinese Government. Continues work at American Locomotive Company.

1944   Leaves Schenectady and returns to Bolton Landing. Finishes studio-workshop.

1946   Large one-man show held at Willard and Buchholz galleries in January with catalogue introduction by William Valentiner.

1947   Traveling retrospective exhibition of Smith's work sponsored by the American Association of University Women. Speaks at Skidmore College and participates in First Woodstock Conference of Artists.

1948   Finishes building long-planned new house at Bolton Landing farm. Takes first teaching position at Sarah Lawrence College.

1950   Receives Guggenheim Foundation fellowship. Smith and Dorothy Dehner separate, and are divorced in 1952.

1951   Receives second Guggenheim fellowship. Lectures at Bennington College and at American University in Washington, D.C.

1952   Continues to lecture at conferences and colleges. Several one-man shows held.

1953   Teaches at University of Arkansas. Has six works represented in Museum of Modern Art traveling exhibition in Europe. In Arkansas, marries Jean Freas, of Washington, D.C.

1954   Teaches at Indiana University. Is delegate to UNESCO's First International Congress of Plastic Arts, held in Venice. Daughter, Rebecca, born April 4.

1955   Teaches at University of Mississippi. Daughter, Candida, born August 12.

1956   Publishes tribute to Julio González in February issue of *Art News*.

1957   Retrospective exhibition held at Museum of Modern Art.

1958   Exhibition of work at XXIX Biennale in Venice.

1961   David Smith and Jean Freas divorced. Smith begins Cubi series.

1962   Invited by Italian Government to produce sculpture for the Fourth Festival of Two Worlds at Spoleto. Smith goes to Voltri, near Genoa, where factories, tools, machine parts, and a work crew are placed at his disposal. In one month he makes twenty-seven sculptures.

1964   One-man show held at Marlborough-Gerson Gallery in New York. Smith is given Brandeis University's Creative Arts Award.

1965   Appointed member of National Council on the Arts. Smith dies following an automobile accident near Bennington, Vermont, on May 23.

II formal writings, speeches, notes

I. Sculpture in a field at Bolton Landing. Photograph by David Smith, c. 1962.

II. *Tanktotem X,* 1960. Steel painted black, blue, red, ocher, white, 61¾ x
45¼ x 24 inches. Achim Moeller Ltd., London. Photograph by David
Smith.

III. *Zig II,* 1961. Steel painted black, red, orange, 100⅝ x 42 x 11¼ inches. Des Moines Art Center; Gift of Gardner Cowles Foundation in memory of Mrs. Florence Call Cowles. Photograph by David Smith.

IV. *11 Books, 3 Apples,* 1959. Stainless steel, 93½ x 31⅜ x 13 inches. From the collection of the Storm King Art Center, Mountainville, New York. Photograph by David Smith.

On Abstract Art

On February 15, 1940, Local 60 of the United American Artists held a forum on abstract art at the Labor Stage, a theater in New York. Years later David Smith recalled the speakers as being himself, Carl Holty, and I. Rice Pereira. Smith's address is an explanation and defense of abstract art to what was probably an audience chiefly attached to the ideals of social realism. Excerpts from the speech were published in the April, 1940, issue of The New York Artist, *organ of the United American Artists.*

The term *abstract* was first used in reference to *Cubism*. That term in America now designates a broad field in painting and sculpture which has made the most significant contribution to contemporary art aesthetics. We may accept the term *abstract* to include Cubism and the later concepts which are based on or related to it. This art language opposes realism per se, the photographic state of nature and conscious literalism.

The fact that the abstract concept is so little understood has no eventual bearing and does not affect its validity. No responsibility can be assumed for uninformed critics who are unable to evaluate its worth and its importance to contemporary social life. The pragmatists and didacticians are too apt in self-defense to set up a hierarchy of standards to conform to their limitations. Their standards, usually based on Italian Renaissance or the new satin nationalism, are an attempt to re-create the past or advocate regionalism through rose-colored glasses. Pragmatists peddle this patent medicine to uninformed minds and even achieve the position of "best seller." The reference is often made that abstract art is not understood by the great American cross-section. That is quite true. It is likewise true that the great cross-section does not understand nonabstract art. Its perceptive faculties have been accustomed to exclude contemporary art that is not represented by magazine covers, or the bronze soldier the town erected to honor the war dead. Possibly there exists an indiscriminate respect for old masters, not because of any understanding but due to the influence of conservatism and its tendency to romanticize and revere the past. Imagination and new ideas cause disturbance to the complacent cross-section, which is accustomed to an art representing the simplest elements of sex, confirmation of a happy experience, or a situation with a moral. Economic conditions for millions of people preclude any interest outside of bare existence when uncertainty of life and constant poverty are dominant. Even the professional "art lover" is usually a generation or more behind the creative artist.

The great cross-section believes that art is something that existed long ago. That art exists today, based on modern concepts, only comes to them second- or third-hand through the design of their ice boxes, advertising, or bric-a-brac. They do not perceive the original creative force yet; the source though unrecognized, and non-profitmaking to the creators, is an important contribution to society.

Certain critics purporting to advance social ideology and the democratic principle have taken issue with the abstract concept, labeling it either unsocial or possibly social in some future society. This position represents an anti-intellectualist view and is reactionary. On common grounds as objectors, we have syndicates of the reactionary press and the so-called Logan Sanity in Art* movement. Super-nationalists and the "blood in mind" fascists object to abstract art on the ground that it is a foreign "ism."

Abstract art is a symbolic treatment of life just as is higher mathematics or music. It is ultra-intellectualist. Appreciation or understanding of any phase of art, past or present, may be a matter of degree and inclination. Even the Italian Renaissance exhibition† was sold with super press-agentry. A guide was required to explain it to one of our leading Hollywood actresses. Whereas a great physicist, on visiting the Picasso show at the same museum, explained in refusing special guide service that it was not necessary since he was well acquainted with most of the Picasso paintings. There is no moral to be drawn; degrees of preference are personal and as such are respected. But condemnation of modern art is too often given over to generalities which are due to a lack of interest and understanding.

The Impressionists were radicals and were given their name in opprobrium by a critic. Cézanne and van Gogh were demons to the critics and cross-section of their time, but today where art is known they are the classic past. In 1905, a group of painters, among whom were Matisse, Braque, and Derain, exhibited paintings based on the belief that art should be primarily an expression of pure aesthetic experience, and that enjoyment of line, form, and color was a sufficient end in itself. These painters were labeled "Wild Beasts," and, a quarter of a century later when they have been accepted as part of our tradition and heritage, trifling educators still condemn their work and sing the glories of the Renaissance hierarchy.

Art is a paradox that has no laws to bind it. Laws set can always be violated. That confuses the pragmatic mind. There may exist conventionalized terminologies and common designations for periods, but no

* An anti-modernist movement of the 1930's.
† An exhibition of paintings lent by the Italian Government to the Golden Gate Exposition held on Treasure Island in 1939.

David Smith

rules bind, either the material substances from which art is made or the mental process of its concept. It is created by man's imagination in relation to his time. When art exists, it becomes tradition. When it is created, it represents a unity that did not exist before.

It is the irrational creative which stands out most distinctively in art and opposes rationalizing efforts. It is from this view that Dutch-Flemish art was superior to Italian Renaissance, that the first Parthenon was superior to the second, that African sculpture in its time was superior to the academies of the Continent. We may sense the force and attempt to describe it, but we will not necessarily understand it. Certain canons of beauty or imagination (which work on the same fundamental principle) are absolute, having common denominators in our associations, but we are ignorant of the laws which determine the number and variety of the more complex combinations. A given form may have relationships with several natural objects, but two forms may raise the relationship to higher powers too complex to tabulate. Yet, the power to tabulate is not necessary in appreciating the beauty of the two forms in relationship, since men of common pursuit in life have the same subconscious registry of those objects. The perception of beauty can thus establish a community between the perceiving and creating mind. We meet on grounds of equality in the unconscious mind. With the exception of the literal message, the communication agrees with the method of the realist concept, although there is a difference in degree.

When we create, we create what we feel. Lesser men and especially critics are afraid of their feelings. They have confusion, they seek solace in words. They are not open to the artist concept—they require conformity to their own.

I may attempt an explanation of Cubism by stating that it was an effort to express the reactions of the sensibility to extend objects in the abstract language of form, but that will not account for a full understanding, nor has any verbal account been able to express all that exists in the concept of Cubist painting and sculpture.

The tradition of our art is international, as are American people, customs, and science. There is no true American art and there is no true American mind. Our art tradition is that of the Western world, which originally had its tradition in the East. Art cannot be divorced from time, place, or science. It has never been dependent on, but is related to, science in the creative sense. The converse is likewise true. Parallel to Impressionism were the Helmholtz and Chevreul theory of light *vibrasm*— Daguerre the painter and physicist, and his machine for reproducing natural images—Darwin the evolutionist, and his theory of natural selection—and the economist and philosopher Marx. Paralleling our own more immediate tradition have been Einstein, with the relativity, space-time theory, and Freud, who has been the greatest single influence on the theoretical side of art, providing an analytical system for establishing the reality of the unconscious, that region of the mind from which the artist derives his inspiration, and proclaims the super reality which permits use of all manifest experience.

Since the introduction of the camera image, and its recent element of color and movement, depiction of the natural image is no longer an art unless created by that machine—the camera—most capable of producing it. The literal message from the painter has seen its day.

The all-inclusive term "abstract" includes Surrealism and tangent schools. It is the language of our time. Within this expression the artist is essentially the instrument, his work stands above him, therefore the interpretation should not be expected of him. Relatively, a great abstract work is like a dream. It presents beauty or its associate, imagination. It does not interpret itself. The dream, like the painting, is the product of both the conscious and unconscious factors of the mind.

I make no particular evaluation of sculpture from painting, since both have common purposes, the only difference being the material use of a dimension—in place of an indicated one.

The abstract artist admits no mystic process, nor do any union members who paint abstractly live in ivory towers. The problems of the abstract artist in a democratic society are common with those of all men of good will. He rejects participation in the present imperialist war and acknowledges his position with organized labor—to keep America out of war, for art and peace can only exist together.

Modern Sculpture and Society

The following piece was written about 1940 at the request of the Federal Art Project for a proposed publication Art for the Millions. *Unpublished at the time, it finally appeared in 1972 in a version edited by Francis V. O'Connor.*

Culture and science are international. The beginning of American culture was foreign, so were her people, her religion, her science, and customs. Europe's culture was foreign. The basis of both cultures came from the East twenty centuries or more ago.

Culture is not a discovery, an authoritative claim or a premeditated act. It is cumulative, built on the past, contributed to by creative forces indigenous to the people, the age. It progresses with free men. It degenerates with dictation.

You have read daily of instances where frenzied medieval sorcery is government-sponsored by book burning, etc. You have seen physicist, psychologist, writer, artist come to our shores as a refugee. These acts represent a people without freedom in politics, art, science, or music. Here, along with suppression of rights, comes dictation for the arts: the aesthetic direction of a culture changed by the dictates of a paperhanger, the fire-kaiser who turns back the clock on everything not lending to the advance of warmaking and destruction of people. On the lower base of an axis triangle we see art awards given to painters of people who listen by radio to fortissimo boasts of a warmongering reactionary. Standing on the fagots of suppression and mass murder we see another dictator trying to force a totalitarian culture. The point of the axis triangle nearest our back represents a country with a feudal culture, whose art has never been free. Without a modern culture, without a freedom to suppress, the need is only to suppress the cries of families whose sons have been killed serving as invaders, or daughters enmeshed in the gears of war production machines.

Art is born of freedom and liberty, and dies of constraint. Fascism contributes race ignominies, suppresses knowledge, erects monuments to destruction, gives laurels to force.

America has outright fascists. It has tendencies. Anti-cultural movements, even in art, advocate sanity in art and are sponsored by the yellowest and most fascist of presses. Certain political and cultural reactionaries who do not openly uphold fascism, possess its tendencies. Culture is international, but so is fascist degeneracy.

The present function of sculpture in our democratic society relies primarily on its relation to architecture. . . . The secondary use may be designated as free-creative. Here the sculpture is conceived independently, for purely aesthetic or fetish reasons. Creative sculpture has always had a definite relationship to the architecture of its period. It has reflected the complexity or simplicity of the forms of its architectural era, and, conversely, architecture has derived a definite influence from sculpture. Illustrating this parallel, Phidias, Michelangelo, Lubetkin represent sculptor and architect both, to varying degrees. The parallel of materials also exists, although we base no aesthetic end in the material itself. This material parallel is evident in early mud building through stone and bronze periods to modern times with the use of alloys, aluminum, and stainless steel. Tools, too, have left the same imprint on sculpture and architecture through the ages to the modern use of fabricated metal in both fields. Both architecture and sculpture have reflected the existing social growth, decadence, science, and cultural pursuits of their time.

The first architecture of man is represented by a cave, in which incised sculptured adornment was included. Throughout man's great periods, architectural concepts have changed by their needs, aesthetic dictates, and scientific advances. Sculptural concepts have changed also.

Modern sculpture—abstract sculpture—is plastically based, as are the plastics of modern architecture. It represents an effort to unite form and form associations into a statement psychologically decisive, intellectually elevating, and physically unified—the purpose being, to create aesthetic enjoyment. Instead of a literary message, the mind reacts to a sequence of related forms; the visual result is derived from actuality by abstract association.

The composition of lines, space, textures forming the structure of a modern building appeals to the eye by an aesthetic principle which most people can accept without knowing the creator's theories relating to composition, or the experiences on which his associations have been formed. From a similar analogy can we base the result in sculpture. Like any progressive attitude in art or science of men of good will, serious and unbiased consideration given to sculpture will further the appreciation of it. A typical bourgeois attitude is to oppose modern sculpture on anti-intellectual grounds. The bourgeoisie have appropriated the anti-intellectual eye to view not only art, but other social-cultural forces as well. Even their notion of realism is limited to a few basic emotional reactions of sentiment and heroics. They accept only the most superficial attitudes of realism. They are interested in one aspect of pictorial representation and that in its most elementary form. While it is true a democratic viewpoint is accorded all people, this bourgeois view is not one which will elevate or stimulate a growing culture.

Abstract sculpture expresses itself in optical aesthetic language. Engineering expresses itself in mathematical language. Both languages are subject to evolution and cultural change. Both art and science are basic forces in that coordination called architecture. Mathematics are creative. Even mathematics, like sculpture, change with time and social concepts.

Modern building cannot disregard sculpture any more than it can mechanics. The sculpture known as abstract is progressive and definitely one of this age, definitely related to modern building and designing, and evident in virtually every present-day object. It is the art of today, and an important contemporary force.

Neolithic, Egyptian, Greek, Roman, Medieval architecture utilized the arts of their time. Vital modern architects will find it necessary to maintain this same cultural concept. Commercial disregard of culture

David Smith

has usually obliged the architect to build on the theory of scarcity and short life. For this reason sculpture included in specifications has often been eliminated.

There is no need for government building, whether federal, state, or municipal, to build on the theory of scarcity or short-term existence. To use the nation's talent and maintain its culture creates a fiscal asset as great or greater than the building itself.

The one government agency to be most highly commended for its use of modern painting and sculpture in relation to its architecture is the WPA. Although dependent on its juries of selection, insufficient appropriations, and whatever committees sponsor the building, it has been able to deliver modern building design with the unity of modern sculpture and painting. Especially noted among its commendable national works are some of its modern housing projects, airports, hospitals, World's Fair buildings, and WNYC broadcasting station. Oftimes the desire for sculpture cannot be fulfilled due to lack of appropriations and layoffs.

It is encouraging that the Treasury Department can build new post offices and can allot a small percentage of costs toward adornment. This represents a somewhat recent development. It is discouraging to see these buildings based on architecture of the past and adorned by art concepts of the past. In due time advances may be made that will permit recognition of modern architecture and sculpture, which have existed outside their world and have been advancing for the last twenty years.

Although the TVA has utilized modern architecture, it has not included sculpture. It would be fitting for TVA to use sculpture in relation to its architecture, which is based on similar concepts. The need would be for sculpture that will uphold the monumental dignity of Norris Dam; sculpture aesthetically as functional as the mechanics at Wheeler, Pickwick, and Gunterville; sculpture with aesthetic elements related to space and contemporary time as are their gantry cranes and gauge houses; sculpture to complement the monolithic majesty of their structures and adjuncts. A sculptured literary message would be out of function.

It is true that reactionaries object to modern sculpture and modern architecture. Yet these reactionaries do not always object on aesthetic grounds alone, but because they object to government power generation and conservation, housing, educational and civic building. Progress in art, progress in society, one accompanies the other and both are decried by Babbitt reactionaries.

The government needs to unify its art direction by creating a ministry of fine arts, to sponsor democracy in art, to enhance its buildings, to preserve its culture, and maintain its artists.

The artists are willing to give to the fullest extent of their abilities, for a living wage. Let them work. It is high time the government takes concerted action for the welfare of its cultural workers, but let it not be alarmed by the cry of that moribund minority who contribute nothing to society and reap golden harvests far greater than they can possibly use.

Sculpture; Art Forms in Architecture—New Techniques Affect Both

One of the few articles written by David Smith expressly for publication, the following piece appeared in Architectural Record *in October, 1940.*

Sculpture has always been dependent upon architecture for its setting, not because it is a "lesser art," but by the very nature of its function and sponsorship. Its purpose has been to lend aesthetic identity to the building's function, either with the mechanics of the interior, or to project or complement the atmosphere created by the exterior. Sculpture not dependent on buiidings proper, but relegated to a setting in the landscape, still maintains this relationship.

Therefore, for aesthetic unity, the architect's building must establish the function of a specific sculpture. Too often the architect misses such unity by making (or allowing) the sculpture to function as a mere billboard. Bromidic quotations, realistic sex imagery, and acts of pretentious idealism too often serve as standard specifications for sculpture, wherein an aesthetic conflict between building and sculpture is naturally introduced. The modern building, by its composition of line, space, and texture, appeals to the eye by definite aesthetic principles; and the sculpture cannot represent a concept alien to the aesthetics of such architecture.

As in architecture proper, so in sculpture, the concept is primary, the material secondary: but there is a constant *interaction* between the two. The secondary or material parallels have existed through the mud, stone, and bronze ages to the present-day period of alloys. And the tools of all ages have left common marks on both.

The aesthetic standards now operative in current sculpture are much the same as those of past periods—namely, that there must be perfect unity between the idea, the substance, and the dimension; that the sculpture be conceived in perfect equilibrium with the related areas. But the

David Smith

thing that differentiates modern sculpture from all its predecessors is its *means* of achieving these aesthetic standards. Never before have the sculptors had so rich and varied a selection of materials, tools, and techniques with which to work. It is the purpose of this paper to summarize these new means.

One of the most important developments in method is the application of welding to metal sculptures; here, by using stock forms, a composite structure may be fabricated with qualities as inherently different from carved or cast pieces as steel framing is from masonry construction. To fabricate a finished piece of sculpture requires a concept in unity with the method, a recognition of the change in forces, a knowledge of the limitations and a respect for the virtues of material and method. This concept already exists in industry and, to a lesser extent, in architecture. Fabricated sculpture is, in a certain sense, "industrialized" in that it uses both industrial methods and materials and makes possible the rapid multiplication of a given piece. As yet uncommon, it seems destined to become relatively important.

Aluminum and its alloys greatly favor sculptural use, by economy of weight, ease of fabrication, and variety of surface treatments. Aluminum's stability and low cost have been attested in architecture and industry. Oxide finishes by anodic treatment are suitable to not too massive sculpture, or to fitted sections. The hard anodic coatings which can only be formed on aluminum are considered to be the most durable, have high corrosion resistance and high dielectric strength. They also produce the best surfaces for dyeing and mineral impigmentation.

Cast aluminum possesses especial economy for the electrodeposition of a variety of metallic plates. It can be plated for exterior use with deposits over one-thousandth of an inch. A dozen or more types of alloy castings are easily worked by hand. In sheet or casts, aluminum responds to fabrication by standard methods.

Stainless steel is ideally suited for sculpture in architecture, but its maximum function will be achieved when it is fabricated from sheets and forms. (This parallels its most important use in architecture and industry.) As a casting metal, its defects are all too evident. In gravity casting it pours thick and slow, making both a bulky and expensive job for sculptural purposes.

Other stainless metals of the copper-nickel alloy type possess similar visual appearance and function best when fabricated.

Bronze casting will probably always serve a useful purpose in sculpture, although the stock bronze in the majority of foundries has become limited to the commercial billet, giving all metal casts much the same color. Statuary bronzes made by the French process, which range in color from red to pale yellow, have fallen from general use, but for art purposes deserve to be rediscovered. Likewise, the oxidation from these bronzes of varying formulas offer greater tonal gradations.

Bronze-sheet alloys for fabricating are obtainable in various color ranges from red (98.10 per cent copper, 1.90 per cent tin) through yellow, red-gray, bluish red, white, to bluish white (25 per cent copper, 75 per cent tin). Similarly, brass alloys of copper and zinc come in wide natural-color ranges. These copper-bearing alloys form oxide finishes from black through red, green, blue to brown by accelerated chemical action and can be fixed by special metal lacquers. To maintain a constant appearance, and for protection from stain to surrounding areas, bronze sculpture should always be protected by lacquer coats.

Steel can be cast, forged, and fabricated to exploit its natural characteristics to denote resistance and tension. It responds to a host of treatments which have possibilities for sculpture. Aesthetic applications wholly untenable in traditional materials are possible.

Sculpture can be built of fabricated steel rods. Lines can indicate form by outline, can confine areas, can maintain their own sculptural import, yet lose nothing by permitting a view of a building or the landscape through the open areas which may represent the inside of the sculptural form. To view a building through the branches of a tree destroys neither the aesthetic value of the tree nor the aesthetic value of the building; they both bear the added interest of associated objects.

Contemporary sculpture has made timid use of color, although it has been an important factor in the best periods of the past. It is obvious that there exists a logic of color in relationship to sculptural form just as there exists a logic in the scale of sculpture. Yet for centuries, bronzes have been dead dark, and marble, dead white. The public has acknowledged its preference for color in articles of everyday use, from hacksaw blades to automobiles. Ironically, the trend behind this change in "industrial design" is accountable to the fine arts, especially to Cubism and later schools which regarded texture, material, and color as aesthetic forces.

Sculpture can be rustproofed by chemical immersion, or sprayed with a chemical solution to produce an insoluble black phosphate, and painted with stable oxide enamels. The form could be brightly painted in winter and softly colored in summer, or repainted in any specified color each decade, or as often as the enamel medium showed weathering.

Steel sculpture sprayed with molten zinc or cadmium, which are both electronegative, thereby affording corrosion resistance by galvanic control, could then be sprayed with harder metals like chromium, Monel, silver, stainless alloys, cobalt, etc. By the molten-spray method, mixed metals can be applied, used as accents or as separate color areas. A steel sculpture sprayed with zinc and accented with copper would exhibit,

David Smith

after buffing, a silver-and-pink-colored granulated surface. This could be held by lacquer or permitted to take on a natural green and white-gray oxide patina.

Useful as a finish for bronze and other metals are the chemically and mechanically stable colors produced by light refraction from a semi-transparent electrodeposit.

A cuprous oxide deposit in violet, blue, green, yellow, orange, and red has been produced by cathodic deposits from alkaline solutions of copper lactate. The color of the deposit is a function of thickness, or plating time. As the thickness of the deposit increases, complete color cycles take place, each cycle building different shades.

Heavy deposits from one-thousandth to five-thousandths of an inch can produce a metallic copper of extremely fine grain, with colors in rich browns of a pigmentary nature. This plate can be buffed and polished, and has a high corrosion resistance.

Ceramic processes have for millenniums been used in architecture and are still important. The most important recent development is the "glass on steel" process of applying vitreous enamels to ingot iron sheets having a common coefficient of expansion. The firing of fabricated sculpture and fitted sections are both possible. So far, one sees the result of this process only on gasoline stations, hamburger stands, and stew pans, but the colors and freedom in application are as flexible and varied as those in the artist's oil palette.

Advanced methods of glass casting and shaping are more important than the use of most synthetic plastics in practically all architectural sculpture, especially in consideration of relative life economy.

Materials with high specific gravity and low tensile strength are still useful in modern architecture. There are times when the exploitation of mass, density, texture, and color common to marble, granite, and stone is aesthetically useful. Oftentimes their contrast with materials possessing opposite qualities is very interesting.

In this same field may be included the plastic counterparts representing various types of concrete. Concrete art forms have largely been but an imitation of the clay model, with their aggregates used to imitate granite and stone. This unimaginative concept of pouring concrete to rigid sculptural form fails to reveal the true nature of the material. As yet it has not suggested new form or new freedom. But concrete is a new material to the sculptor, and (it is well to remember) it suffered quite as badly in the architect's hands until it was freed by Freyssinet and Maillart.

Although sculpture has by definition always exploited natural light, use of artificial lighting as a basic element of design has never been practical until recent times. It still remains a development requiring new mechanics and concepts. The use of varying intensities, types of light, and controlled beams offers amazing potentialities. Objects projected, objects moving in controlled light, or moving light on static objects have possibilities yet to be investigated sculpturally. Not only can light be used in new relationship to material form, but it can be developed as an independent form. Projected light naturally functions best in a darkened field. It has a limited use, but an important and distinctive one.

Physical movement in sculpture also offers possibilities, especially when it is used as a basic element of design as Calder, Brancusi, and Man Ray, among others, have done. *The Miracle* of Brancusi, when shown at the Museum of Modern Art, was rotated by a quiet low-gear operation, turning the sculpture with a smoothness and precision impossible to obtain if the onlooker had been forced to reverse the viewing process and walk around the sculpture. An amusing (and effective) example of physical motion in sculpture is to be seen in Walter Dorwin Teague's *Cycle of Production* at the Ford exhibit at the New York Fair. Here highly stylized figures go through a cycle of highly stylized motions illustrating the various steps in motorcar manufacture.

Medals for Dishonor

Following are catalogue statements for the series Medals for Dishonor, exhibited at the Willard Gallery, November, 1940.

1. Propaganda for War

The rape of the mind by machines of death—the Hand of God points to atrocities. Atop the curly bull the red cross nurse blows the clarinet. The horse is dead in this bullfight arena—the bull is docile, can be ridden.

The speakers part the mind and offer red apples while Radio parts the ether with shrieks and emotional bombings. The corny trumpet leaves behind sour footnotes, the walking speaker spews ballast. Behind the nurse hang wires heavy laden with atrocity stories—burned nuns—dog eats child—death sells hoover apples—torn bodies and spilt milk.

The web is spun, the stage is set—not for the fish story of Jonah but for the present fish story—Propaganda. The female auxiliary—the chorus girl—helps by what she is most able.

David Smith

2. The Fourth Estate

The Free Press—whose presses run with oil and sex—whose presses are gummed by patent medicine—whose censors, the Power Trust, wield scissors of every known kind—whose hand has wrapped five columns from the citadel of justice around the index finger—which has tied with ragged knots the brunhildean key to sex and fish.

The formula stories roll—the well-oiled banners fly with herring bones and tipped scales—fish and windy gloved hands under the flags in a wrong-way breeze—inverted pawnballs—the oil can and the daisy. Liberty is strung.

3. Munition Makers

Patched skeletons take up their old duties—the shellbearer, the spearman, the shepherd, the cripple.

The banner of death-dollars flies from the stub of a medieval soldier's arm. An ancient coin is held aloft—"the pen is mightier than the sword," but the soldier still clings to the tommygun.

The antediluvian land tortoise comes forward with low-hanging buttocks. From the imprint of past ages emerge shellholes and ancient coins marked by the gain of the merchants of death.

4. Diplomats: Fascist and Fascist Tending

Amidst the field of broken umbrella blossoms stands the balancing act by the muscleman and his accomplice. The trained seal does the ball act. For the parade the torchlight is represented by two faces under the same high hat.

A veiled rat with pawnball tail is atop the pork barrel wherein the porkers kiss. There is danger that the muscleman may have his achillean heel nipped by the gila.

The deadliest guns are not in the field but in the chancelleries!

5. Private Law-and-Order Leagues

Black Legion—Klan—Bund—fordstream of Americanism. From the pulpit the noose hangs—their christ was not a jew.

Hoods are on the horizon. The tree has roots and bore fruit for vultures. The sacred cow with pumphandle tail rides high on the moon.

Liberty and classic foo: Women are caught in the act in the house of girdles, or tethered in bushes with a sack over the head, or peep from behind the flag still carrying the nation hatchet—the hounds lick and smell.

The superamerican rises from the pit of medievalism and by the grace of modern industrialism is aiming directly at you.

6. War-exempt Sons of the Rich

The shape suggests a large coin comprised of smaller coins:

The monkey fan dances on war drum with carnival lights.

The polo boy does his bit—tilts at the birdhouse windmill—the lady of the sun cools air and land for him—the dog follows.

The cafe lady pours herself into her own cocktail glasses to be auctioned for thirst quenchers—we do much for charity—we have our milk funds, fall out of bed, catch greased pigs.

The entertainers must be fed from rubber bottles.

On the backs of worker and soldier rest the joys of exempt sons— the cherries swing 'round the clock, bluebirds fly away with the topper—the dial is tuned, the needle points, the sign is one way— the beribboned knife cuts pieces—the family fortune increases.

The Greek on this medal is slang for soft cookies.

7. Cooperation of the Clergy

War fatalism of all the clergy—deniers of Christ's hebrew ancestry— acceptors of religious dominance over fascist conquest.

Angel Gabriel blows the tuba, wearing Coughlin's glasses—while various sects in unison man the anti-aircraft into the heavens—not to kill mankind but to shoot merely ducks—to incite the lame in mind.

The chalice cups and the rights of sacrament—to drink the blood and partake of the body. Tentacles hold down the cloth and keep the book open.

8. Death by Gas

The specter sprays heavy gas—the mother has fallen—flaming and eaten lungs fly to space where planets are masked. Two bare chickens escape in the same apparatus. The death venus on wheels holds aloft the foetus who, from environment, will be born masked.

The immune goddess in the boat hangs to the handle of a tattered umbrella. . . . She wears a chastity mask and blows her balloon. The peach pits were saved in the last war.

9. Bombing Civilian Populations

The Stuka storks fly high and drop eggs. The statue has been blown apart revealing a thirteenth-century concept of a Caesarean.

David Smith

The baby is on the bomb—the bomb is in the highchair—the earth is torn and cracked—the buildings are shattered.

10. Sinking Hospital and Civilian Refugee Ships

The cruiser has scored—the spirits of the sunken hold aloft the fish from the sea—Venuses whose hair is seaweed float upward to meet the newcomers.

The hospital ship founders—the drowned family gathers in a lifeboat. Schools of fish have little to learn from mankind. Man is tentacled by the sea-terror.

11. Death by Bacteria

Gloved hands hold test tubes emitting froth of bacteria disseminated from the music harp symbolizing death music. The foetus is balanced on the harp column—rats for cultures—germs pour from flasks—music bars provide places for notes and rat dung to rest. From a flask the culture eats the earth in furrows—the dead lie in seas marked by common crosses.

The coffin plows on toward the skeleton of past histories and the molds of excavated wonders.

12. Reaction in Medicine

Complete and replete in sections of science—the surgeon performs an operation on the body instrument—the music is in shreds—Faith sabotaged—old ways discarded.

Science on the lookout—Death climbs a wall. Beyond the amphitheater wall lie the contorted bodies of those in need.

13. Elements Which Cause Prostitution

The land is cushioned—the bowl has the sponge—the fern has futility —the anchor of hearts is ashore—the vulture disembowels. Salvarsan needles to the shamefully stricken—the wine is spilled—both eagles fly to the rescue.

Shamefully she stands knee deep in classic water—her body eaten and pitted with holes. The preventative balloon trails sandbags. The body stands dissected by extant medieval concepts.

14. Food Trust

The destroyers of natural resources—who burn coffee and corn— dump potatoes in rivers—burn cotton—put kerosene on oranges—to keep prices high—to profiteer while those who once produced starve.

The floating sections of sanitation—broken female dresser and pawn specter.

Boiled roots are foul with gas—the girl is covered with plague of snakes—the boy is naught but bone.

The plow lies fallow—the horse unseeded—the cross on the tabernacle is tied with bowknots. It is infected with vermin, vermin.

15. Scientific Body Disposal

The song of sewage—dust to dust returneth, and life to food returneth —mass bombing and mass murder. Those who are meant not to be can be used—as fertilizer, as food for propaganda—transposed through modern industrial channels like pulpwood.

Science, chemistry, and production line can dispose of masses of cadavers, turning them to good use—through the channels back to the cornucopia which again bears wheat.

The circle repeats—the table again bears food.

The Sculptor's Relationship to the Museum, Dealer, and Public

The First Woodstock Conference of Artists was held at Woodstock, New York, on August 29, 1947. Smith's address was followed by a brief question-and-answer period.

I was a member of a steelworkers' union that fights for you and watches over your welfare. An artists' organization is an entirely different thing in the sense that its problems are different, but nevertheless there are certain grounds that everybody has in the straight battle. There are economic factors that benefit all of us, in any equity organization or brotherhood. The artist's product varies according to his individual ability. His concept and concept-battle is pretty much of an individual affair. The economic battle is much the same for all creative artists.

Exhibiting with museums and societies offers little economic salvation. In most societies and some museums an exhibition fee is levied, which when added to the expense of packing, shipping, and insuring makes the artist pay dearly to show his child. The salvation appears to be in the business contact known as the dealer. But there are not enough

David Smith

V.   Left to right: *Voltron XIX*, 1963; *Voltri-Bolton VI*, 1962; *Voltron IV*, 1963; *Voltri-Bolton X*, 1962; *VB XXII*, 1963; *Voltri-Bolton VII*, 1962; *Voltron XIII*, 1963 (partly hidden). Photograph by Dan Budnick, 1963.

VI. *Zig VII,* 1963. Steel painted cream, red, blue, 94¾ inches high x 100⅜ inches wide. Estate of the artist. Photograph by David Smith.

VII. *Wagon I,* 1964. Steel painted black, 87⅝ x 120 x 63⅞ inches. The
National Gallery of Canada, Ottawa. Photograph by David Smith.

VIII.   *Cubi XXVIII,* 1965. Stainless steel, 108 inches high x 112⅛ inches
wide. Norton Simon, Inc., Museum of Art, Los Angeles. Photograph
by David Smith.

dealers to represent the large number of exhibiting artists. The number of dealers is proportioned to the number of people who buy art, not to the number of artists who need dealers.

Some dealers act as patrons. They carry nonsalable artists in whom they have faith. But because they derive no income except from sales, there is a limit to the length of time and the number of nonselling artists a dealer can carry. Some actually encourage the artist to new heights in his own direction. Others encourage the artist to meet some fancied or real public demand, and/or provide contracts for converting so-called fine art into advertising. Due to the odds, artists usually solicit dealers. Artists can submit works to museums, but they cannot successfully solicit purchases from either collectors or museums.

Most dealers work on a 33⅓ per cent commission plan. This means that after the dealer advertises, publishes the catalogue, mails the announcements, pays the gallery help, rent, and utilities for three weeks or more, the exhibit sales must come near $3,000 to even the score. It usually costs the artist one-third or more of his sale price to produce the work. Herein sculpture differs materially in that the cost of production nears 50 per cent of the selling price. Then, too, few dealers have space or preference for it.

The artist's labor, or wage, is from 16⅔ per cent to 33⅓ per cent of the sales price. This is not a standard used in determining art prices, but an average based upon questions to both painters and sculptors. The wage per hour for art work is usually below that of organized labor. There are exceptions that exceed these figures, but these are a fair average. Even the much sought-for security of university teaching pays less than skilled union labor.

With these figures in mind, is it any wonder that artists are galled by the museum practice of deducting 10 to 15 per cent of the sale price of a work? This divine right is usually backed by some logical reason relating to the budget or what the museum does for the artist. We artists live on sales to museums. The museum has just as much need for the artist as the artist has for the museum. This cut-rate policy can be eliminated by concerted action on the part of artists. Museums usually buy through dealers—so add up the dealer's third, the one-third or more cost of productions, the museum's 10 to 15 per cent deduction, and you have a possible 1⅔ minimum to 23⅓ maximum per cent of margin for your labor and creation.

Private collectors usually acquire work before museums. They account for the earliest and greatest number of acquisitions in the contemporary field, probably not because of greater appreciation or astuteness but because one mind instead of ten decides. Museums usually have well-informed and appreciative curators, but purchases must be approved by trustees who are quite often more concerned with money values than art values.

Whatever hope we have economically lies with state sponsorship or with private collectors, especially the younger collectors who, for the most part, are professional people. Certain economic assistance can be gained from sculptural and mural commissions, but it is doubtful that any great art or revolutionary concepts will be developed in their execution. Such work approaches commercial standards—preconceptions of it having been made by minds of less vision than those of the artists.

I don't believe in competitions, unless remuneration is made for submission of entries. Exhibition prize money smells of royal condescension. Prize money should be equally divided among the creators of the works exhibited. I don't believe in exhibiting in any museum that levies exhibition fees and handling charges. I don't believe in artists' donations to museums. I don't believe the artist has any professional duty to the public; the reverse is the case. It is the artist who possessed the concept. It is the public's duty to understand.

Art is always an expression of revolt and struggle. Progressive man and progressive art are identified with the struggle, intellectually and anthropologically. That is our history as artists. That is man's history as a primate. The terms "active beauty" and "imagination" are interchangeable. They are part of the creative concept, a basis of fine art, a state forever disturbing to the philistine mind constantly at rest.

The artist's creative vision cannot go so far beyond the rest of the world that he is not understandable. He is limited by his time. He is dependent upon the past, but he is a contributing factor to the character of his time. His effort is to contribute a unity that has not existed before. The receptor must to some degree be able to put himself in the artist's place. This participation can be unconscious, and free, and pleasurable. If the participation is conscious during the transportation, the participant becomes a critic, in the fine sense.

Ernst Kris states that no art has a homogeneous audience. The audience is always stratified in degrees of understanding. There are those who come close, those who remain on the fringe, and those who pretend.

Franz Boas, in summing up the art of primitive people, wrote as follows: "I believe we may safely say that in the narrow field that is characteristic of each people, the enjoyment of beauty is quite the same as among ourselves, intense among the few, slight among the mass."

Fine art is unrelated to our finance-capital-culture. The instincts of aggression and self-destruction are more dominant than beauty and imagination. The creative artist's life has always been a battle. That is progress and the continuing state of evolution.

David Smith

Questions and Discussion:

What form of state sponsorship of art is good for the artist?

We were on the road to state sponsorship at one time. It developed in accordance with the artists' ability, skill, and common need. I think the direction was all right. But when they started to cut payment to the artist down, that was wrong. Everybody was working, but then you couldn't eat on it and do the work at the same time. You cannot start out with a perfect thing and I wouldn't know where to adjust the wage scale in proportion to the present cost of living now. But we had the thing going to where there were good administrators, and a certain basis was established, a recognition of what was required and what the artist was able to do. I don't see that sort of thing again for quite a while.

Don't you feel that one reason state sponsorship of art failed was because not enough people understood? Some awfully good work was done under the program, but simply not enough of the public understood the thing. And that's why it failed, because, after all, politicians will listen to reason.

There are never enough who understand, but to expect people to understand all phases of art is impossible. Artists come from all backgrounds, have different reactions to life, and no two create the same way, and all of it has to be represented. The government has to take a strong stand on art, as it does with the educational aspects of agriculture, etc. There should be a state project to encourage the production of art of all kinds, and the best of its kind. The public can be helped to understand it through an aggressive program of popularization, through people and channels of education that reach out to the public. But today there is no commercial backing, and people have to acquire this understanding themselves for there's no real plan afoot for the broad understanding of art by the people. It isn't reasonable to assume that the work of an artist is immediately accepted by people who listen to the radio and read comic books or by the general cross-section of the country.

If the painter has a difficult time with the public, the sculptor's plight is even worse. What do you have to offer as a hope to sculptors?

The hope isn't much . . . the cost is greater than painting. He has to go on working and fighting for public support of his work. He isn't in it for money, if he were he wouldn't be one. His only salvation, I think, is state sponsorship, another WPA or whatever we had in the various letter combinations. That's what I'd like to see on a reasonable merit and production basis. I haven't thought that over so much. It should be thought about and also talked over with any union, with Equity, and other opinions should be asked.

Design for Progress—*Cockfight*

The following statement on arc welding was written about 1947.

In free creative design, usually only one creation exists. Industrially speaking, this corresponds to the development project or the design model. Since this design (viz. sculpture) has a visual purpose wholly based on a matter of aesthetics, there is little technical data involved in the paper or project. The use of arc welding to develop aesthetics is strictly twentieth century. My project to the best of my knowledge is the first all arc-welded sculpture to be acquired by an American museum of art. I submit it not as a project of aesthetics made for the competition but one which was made a year before the competition, using arc welding purely because it functioned as the best method in arriving at the desired aesthetic ends.

I might say that to use arc welding for aesthetics, technical processes and knowledge must be so well absorbed that control is subconscious or, in other words, the action must proceed on an involuntary basis. The technical procedures must flow so freely that they in no way interfere with the mind's vision or art concept.

My arc welding, as well as all other metal working processes, proceeds automatically. I expect perfection and precision from my materials—my mind is involved in the creation of form. Arc welding is a free and natural medium to me. It is the most desirable method of joining metal—here in sculpture—just as it was when I welded tanks, destroyers, and locomotives at the American Locomotive Works. My materials on this project are the same as I used on locomotives, i.e., no. 5 and no. 7 Lincoln rod and a Lincoln generator.

While arc welding builds the machinery which rolls our present-day industrial culture, the machines will be discarded from wear or obsolescence to be remelted for new developments. But future generations will always be able to see arc-welded, signed and dated sculpture still retained in museum collections. History has been able to show the progressive development of past cultures by the art which represented that age. My project represents an aesthetic contribution in the collection of the City Art Museum of St. Louis purchased on art merit. That this sculpture *Cockfight* is all arc-welded steel was the preference of the artist. This preference was dictated by the fact that arc-welding fabrication was the most functional way of arriving at a given aesthetic end.

The aesthetic standards governing the modern concept of sculpture

David Smith

are much the same as those of past periods: namely, that there must be a perfect unity between the idea and the substance.

This project is not a historic departure, for art throughout the ages has been made from the same materials and borne the same tool marks as industry and architecture. This truth is evident from man's history through mud, stone, bronze ages all the way to our present alloy age.

But never before has sculpture had so rich and varied a selection of materials, tools, and techniques to work with. The need to survive has always been the primary motive in man. The tools for survival were naturally the first development. But the natural art instinct in man was manifest in the design and decoration of those tools. In this industrial age it is only natural that art utilize the advance of industry. Historically it has, and herewith I present art by arc welding.

The arc-welding fabrication of sculpture has caused certain changes in aesthetic concepts, just as it has in industrial design. The aim is no longer to imitate a casting. The art concept must be in unity with the method—a recognition of the change of forces, knowledge of the material and respect for the virtues of the method, and a creative vision of the yet unlimited possibilities which the new method has opened.

I first used arc welding as a conceptual means in sculpture in 1937. As far as I know that was its first use by an artist in the fabrication of his own creative output. In the past ten years my sculpture has been acquired by the Whitney wing of the Metropolitan Museum of Art, New York City; the Detroit Museum; the Museum of Modern Art, New York City; the City Art Museum of St. Louis; as well as by numerous art galleries and private collections. My work in this media has been exhibited in practically every museum in the United States. I have had fourteen one-man shows in galleries and museums. For ten years the Willard Gallery, at 32 East 57th Street, has been my agent and dealer. Under the sponsorship of Mr. John W. Higgins, an exhibition of my work consisting of thirty-seven pieces will be shown at the John Woodman Higgins Armory (Worcester Presteel Company), Worcester, Mass.

This arc-welded steel sculpture called *Cockfight* is not to be considered a novelty project. The museums who buy my work and the critics who compliment it are not particularly interested in the technical process; their interest is purely that of aesthetic appreciation. Being called a modernist, an abstractionist, and admitting to an advanced conception in aesthetics, I was forced to find a technical process which functioned with the advanced art concept.

I herewith submit the use of arc welding in fine art.

Two Poems

The Golden Eagle . . . A Recital

(to be spoken only by one who is politically white blue yellow or
black, who hath not touched women, and who hath not eaten flesh of
animals or fish)

Marvel! Where was it ever before said such a thing was done
Have I not filled my temples with thy spoils
Have I not made thee many and great buildings of stone from far lands
Are not the towers guarded by flying phallus cannot the rape of maid-
 ens, the suckers of blood the crushers of bone throughout the ages
Have I not made these towers with iron from Mesabi and Lebanon
With molten glass from the heat of man's brow the earth around
With granite from Sinai
With blood from the greatest gutters
With obelisks from Abeu
Have I not lighted these wonders with tungsten from China
Sacrificed virgins to bells coolies to ore
Have I not launched boats upon the sea to bring the finest of oils
And into the air birds for bulbs—fragrant in bloom
Have I not confounded all who resisted by designs
And chastisest the foreigners—and bow their backs forever

Robinhood's Barn

Little nodes from big nodes spring
And make great the progeny thereof
Paters love and the transfixed gate
Sold shad that should be for free
Rise and shine come out of the wall
Approach the temple by going forth
Men are vermin slithering on Sekhets belly
Behold the staff which blossoms
I am Tem the tree
The might of my strength is in my hand
Lonesome and blue here I stand
I am the dog headed ape in a golden palm
With a golden hind, parting the curtains
Looking for the tunnel to Memphis.
Hoping to part the curtains for a look at Memphis.

From *Tiger's Eye,* June, 1948.

David Smith

Statement

David Smith presented this statement at a New York Herald Tribune *forum held with the New York City Board of Education on March 19, 1950. Brief as it is, it represents an important development in Smith's thought on art.*

I believe that my time is the most important in the world—that the art of my time is the most important art—that the art before my time has made no immediate contribution to my aesthetics since that art is history, explaining past behavior, but not necessarily offering solutions to my problems. Art is not divorced from life. It is dialectic. It is ever changing and in revolt with the past. It has existed in the minds of free men for less than a century. Prior to this, the direction of art was dictated by minds other than the artist for exploitation and commercial use. The freedom of man's mind to celebrate his own feeling by a work of art parallels his social revolt from bondage. I believe that art is yet to be born and that freedom and equality are yet to be born.

If you ask why I make sculpture, I must answer that it is my way of life, my balance, and my justification for being.

If you ask for whom do I make art, I will say that it is for all who approach it without prejudice. My world, the objects I see are the same for all men of good will. The race for survival I share with all men who work for existence.

What I Believe About the Teaching of Sculpture

The following address was given at a panel on the Teaching of Sculpture, held at the Midwestern University Art Conference in Louisville, Kentucky, October 27, 1950.

The concept of art can be known only by following the path of the creator who conceives it, not by the analysis of the critic or the words of art history.

To the serious students I would not teach the analysis of art or art history—I would first teach drawing; teach the student to become so fluent that drawing becomes the language to replace words. Art is made without words. It doesn't need words to explain it or encourage its making.

Period art is related to the writing, music, and the social scene and demands a living emotional understanding by individual experience. Most of the critic-historians use word conclusions not based on the creative artist's directives. The accent on conclusions is too much stressed in our study.

I would stress anthropology such as Boas's study of the creative art in the history of man, psychology as it depicts the function of the creative mind. In writing I would include the study of Joyce's work, such as *Finnegans Wake,* wherein the use of words and relationships function much as in the process of the creative artist's mind. Music must be included. It transmits aural relationships that are akin to the artist's creative form directives. I could cite Schönberg in this instance.

The myth of man is covered by the joint fields of anthropology and psychology. Not only does the myth of man control many things in the creative art field, but within the art stream exists the artist's myth as well. The whole language of art, the history of art, is not spoken in words but represented visually.

The way I would teach art demands more freedom than the average academic institution permits. It would demand a great change in the present archaic educational routine. It would be based more on individual need and less on mass production, the repetition of curriculum setup. It would require the latitude of full days.

I would first start the teaching of art by doing, developing fluency in expression. I would teach contemporary art, contemporary concepts —because that is the world the student lives in—before any accent was made on the history of art.

The history of art is an important but subservient aspect in the making of art. I would require that it be by visual response, based on the understanding of doing as the true way. The present bone-dry art history is fractious and individually prejudiced, lacking social and psychological interpretation, even subject to change by the most recent excavations or excavations to come. Most of the conclusions and clichés belong too much to the pragmatists who wrote them.

I make no separate provision for the cause of sculpture apart from painting. The preference governing actual material is personal. The concept in either art comes from the expression of emotion and thought. The difference in technical pursuit does not change the mind's reaction to form. Accent on any aesthetic difference is the prerogative of the layman. In my own case I don't know whether I make some pieces as painted sculpture or paintings in form.

After the fluency of drawing is attained, and the will to produce an aesthetic result, certain technical activities must be introduced. For the feeling of form develops with technical skill. The means for fulfillment must be provided strictly on the individual's need. Imaginative form will not develop with the acquisition of skill or high technique. But at a point in student development one piece in bronze is worth more than all books and all teachers. The filing, finishing, patination of a rough bronze to completion is a maturing point. There is probably not a college city in America where decent casting cannot be obtained if the problem is planned.

I do not demand that all students be artists, but I would insist that they study that way. I would emphasize the artist's position in society, the influences and traditions, and the world in which the student must fight for survival. I would direct him to literature, music, anthropology, wherein these fields presented aesthetic stimulation to complement his own work.

I would tell him the limits of his audience and that his world is no different from the world for any man of ideas, nor for that matter relatively no more different from the artist's world for the past hundred years.

But to point out the need let me quote [Franz] Boas: "No people known to us, however hard their lives, may spend all their time and energies in the acquisition of food and shelter—nor do those who live under more favorable conditions, and who are free to devote to other pursuits the time not needed for securing their sustenance, occupy themselves with purely industrial work or idle away the days in indolence. Even the poorest tribes have produced work that gives them aesthetic pleasure—and those whom a bountiful nature or greater wealth of invention has granted freedom from care, devote much of their energy to the creation of works of beauty."

There is a need for art. As well as ego satisfaction, the artist has a social obligation to produce to the fullest extent of his ability. It is society's duty to make the effort to understand before it takes an active prejudice. At present he is confronted with a limited audience and a hostile majority, especially with all the excuses found to be anti-intellectualist amid social upheaval and perpetual war.

To the majority there is no need for art on the basis that creative art is produced. We live in a hypocritical world. Our ideologies are only pretensions. We are afraid to be serious, introspective or contemplative. Everything must jump, joke, quickly change scene. Our words in the hands of advertisers have lost their meaning. Books must be digested.

There is still an innate natural sense of beauty in all people. Aesthetic pleasure is released by natural forms, the song of a bird, the flow of a landscape, the formation of clouds, the roll of water; various natural phenomena all possess aesthetic value, but they are not art nor is the imitation thereof, in diminution or enlargement, art. Television and technicolor may even supplant this natural sense of beauty.

But the artist will still state his truth. The artist reprojects the vision in his mind; he possesses it. The vision represents the sum total of his experience. It is part myth, part dream, part reality. It shows the state of inspiration which Plato termed "productive madness." Every swipe of the brush, every stroke of the chisel, every segment applied in construction, is a revisualization, a finality, a simplification of reordered reality, raised to a symbolic level.

Ernst Kris states that productive madness is a specific state of ego control in which unconscious material is freely accessible and, in Freud's own words, "rises to a preconscious level." The subjective experience is that of a flow of thoughts or images driving toward expression in word or shape. We may sense the irrational creative force and attempt to describe it, but we will not necessarily understand it. Certain canons of beauty or imagination, which work on the same fundamental principle, are absolute, having common denominators in our associations, but we are ignorant of the laws which determine the number and variety of the more complex combinations. . . .

The student of art comes with a calling. The underlying directive may be from various motives. He may be directed to art by the opportunities to express sublimations, gratifications, substitutions, constructions or destructions. His impulses do not differ from those of other productive men who follow the same general principle. He is like the clergyman, the prizefighter, the poet, the scholar—the odds are terrific against financial respectability, yet since the ego is greater than the promise of riches, these brothers, men with the call, will always be with us. Despite the retrogressive society, art, artists, and particularly the avant-garde are increasing. Apathy has bred an extremely hardy lot in America.

Clement Greenberg states: "Painting was freed from sculpture by impressionism. Sculpture was freed from the monolith by cubism." The freedom of man's mind to celebrate his own feeling by a work of art parallels his social revolt from bondage. I believe the time now is the greatest time in the history of man to make art. It is the only world I know, it is the only one I can live in.

Progress Report on Guggenheim Fellowship, 1950–1951, and Application for Renewal, February, 1951

I would like another productive Guggenheim year, to complete a two-year program.

David Smith

I want to have this two-year project exhibited at an important museum. If this cannot be accomplished, I will try to show the collective two years at the Willard and Buchholtz galleries jointly, as I did in my ten-year retrospective showing.

I feel that this maturity and impetus will help me start to sell work or establish a position that will lead to a teaching job.

ACCOMPLISHMENT I

The first nine months to date have been the most fluent and productive period of my career.

Completion in this time of thirteen works, all in metal, several six feet in height, one being a four-figure group, the others larger and with more conceptual depth than previous work, makes it almost a certainty that I will complete the eighteen or more works as planned in the twelve-month period.

Completion of thirty full-page drawings in ink and color, all relating to sculptural concepts for continued work. Four of these drawings are shown now at the Willard Gallery group show, four are included in an exhibition at the University of Iowa.

Nine fellowship pieces will be shown at the Willard Gallery, March 27 to April 21. One six-foot piece called *The Fish* will be exhibited in the Sculpture Annual at the Whitney Museum, March 15, 1951.

The May issue of *Art News* will carry an article by Elaine de Kooning on the various stages involved in the fellowship work, *The Cathedral,* describing the method, the concept, the studio, my intent, and presenting a general evaluation of my career.

I sold one work, netting $333.00, in the Museum of Modern Art exhibition for the year of 1951—none in 1952.

ACCOMPLISHMENT II

Explanation of aesthetic intent (as it relates to the new directions shown in *24 Greek Y's, 17 h's, 36 Bird Heads,* etc.):

Before letters—consequently words—existed, the artist-sculptor made symbols of objects. The objects depicted were identity memories that came purely from the artist's mind. The pragmatists later made words and, to this day, turn these symbols against the artist by demanding the "what does it mean" explanation when the formation all along was of artist origin and represented a statement requiring only visual response and association.

This premise I relate to research in cuneiform, the Sumero-Akkadian style of writing, and other Mesopotamia Valley cultures; the origins of

Chinese writing; my own interpretations of Polynesian symbol writing or records. This has not been scholarly research or scientific, but romantic, an interest of relaxation from labor; but like every influence of an artist's life—interpreted into his own creative outlook.

In these sculptures I have sought object identity by symbols, demanding the return to symbol origin before these purities were befouled by the words.

I have used repetition, and rearrangement, for visual acceptance only; I mean them to be accepted by the tenets of art appreciation, requiring no code or specially trained response other than the love of art.

I was trained in the Cubist world concept, but before I could read, had pondered over cuneiform. My first conscious interests were the illustrations in the Bible of cuneiform, which impressed me more than the word language I later learned to read. I have always been more Assyrian than Cubist.

The other works, *The Forest, The Fish, The Letter, Song of the Landscape,* etc., carry out my mainstream concept in celebration of the beauties from my own point of view.

ACCOMPLISHMENT III

As far as I know I am the first American to work sculpture directly in steel and like materials.

My first one-man show was at the East River Gallery in New York showing works of 1935, 1936, and 1937.

During the next ten years I had thirteen one-man shows at the Willard Gallery and Minnesota's University Gallery, Skidmore College Gallery, Olivet College Gallery, Albany Institute of Art, Munson-Williams-Proctor Institute, etc.

During this time my work has been shown in almost every museum in the United States and in Hawaii, Canada, and Puerto Rico, and included in numerous traveling exhibitions.

In small towns without museums, my work has been shown in libraries, clubs, and halls under the sponsorship of the American Association of University Women's clubs from coast to coast. Typical were towns such as Glens Falls, New York; Terre Haute, Indiana; Santa Fe, New Mexico. This traveling exhibition is now in its third year.

Included in ten best shows of 1946 and listed in four to lead 1946 by *Art News.* Cited as the leading American sculptor by Milton Brown in *Magazine of Art* and Clement Greenberg in *The Nation* and *Horizon* (London).

Included in permanent collections of Whitney, Modern, Detroit, St. Louis museums, etc., as well as private collections.

ACCOMPLISHMENT IV

Since the ten-year retrospective show at the Buchholtz and Willard galleries in 1946, a specific account of showings has not been kept. As an example I submit my dealer's report for 1948 showing seventeen different exhibits.

Have won no prizes, scholarships, or awards.

Have maintained the same dealer's interest since 1937, not by sales but by the dealer's faith. My only sales for 1949 were both to other artists: Robert Gwathmey, painter, purchased *Low Landscape* for $200 direct; Gina Knee (Mrs. Alex Brook), painter, purchased *House in Landscape* through my dealer for $750. Dealer's interest netted $250 for the year; my income was $700. My expenditure for sculpture for 1949 was $2,178, partly met by teaching sculpture at Sarah Lawrence College ($1,900). However, I am in last year at the college, being only a substitute teacher.

PLAN FOR WORK

On the basis of completed work, I hope for continuance in 1951–1952.

A. Five works (steel) related to letter symbols (*24 Greek Y's, 17 h's,* etc.);

B. Ten works following poetic sculptural interpretations (such as *The Forest, Star Cage,* etc.);

C. Three lost-wax-process bronzes (purchased 225 pounds pig bronze);

D. Sixty 19 × 25 inch drawings, studies for sculptural work;

E. Fourteen steel-plate etchings 12×14 inches—15×16 inches in size (editions to be printed outside)—all preliminary development work, both aesthetic and manual, have already been done on four plates. The essential abstract forms are sawed out of steel plate, then etched, engraved, hammered, chiseled, etc.—whatever is necessary by form requirement—the individual parts then welded to a bed plate before printing.

REFERENCE NOTE

A, B, C projects require steel and bronze, much of which is in stock, and, as the Terminal Iron Works receive quotas from steel suppliers, this project will not be curtailed due to lack of material.

REFERENCE NOTE

D and E. Metal working is hard and dirty. Sometimes I like to clean up at night, pursue lighter work. D and E projects represent lighter work, evening work, and are only to be considered as supplementary.

Plan for Work

My notebooks are full of sketches for work to be done.

By the number of shows and some two hundred works to date, you can see that my work is steady; only time is needed.

I ask for your faith in my statement that I will produce twenty sculptures in this year. Maybe it will be eighteen, or possibly thirty like I did in 1946. In any event it will be serious. I average twelve hours a day at work. It is my way of life.

My workshop is in Bolton Landing. The tools and materials for work are available here. Both my peace with the world and my materials are located in this area. It is where I can work best.

Extra Activity

I ordinarily cannot take part in relatively unpaid activity, but under the fellowship, participated in the following:

Third Woodstock Art Conference (Woodstock, New York). Panel chairman for Exhibitions and Juries session.

Midwestern University Art Conference (Louisville, Kentucky). Delivered paper on "A Contemporary Sculptor's Concept."

Corcoran Regional Exhibition—sculpture juror. Lecture with slides of 1950–1951 work entitled "For Whom Do You Make Sculpture?" Wrote foreword for Corcoran catalogue.

American University (Washington, D.C.). Lecture with slides of 1950–1951 fellowship work entitled "A Sculptor's Concept." In this lecture slides were shown of work from 1933 to 1951.

Miscellaneous Notes

The fellowship fund was supplemented by one sale of $333.00 net of a work entitled *Billiard Player* to Roy Neuberger from the Museum of Modern Art exhibition. This was the only sale during 1950 and 1951.

I purchased a Rolleiflex camera and exposure meter, and recorded in color over 100 works from 1933 to 1951.

I purchased a 4 × 5 Bush Pressman camera with tripod for recording work, and consequent 8 × 10 enlargements.

Due to my isolation it seemed necessary to purchase the camera, for shop record and for publicity.

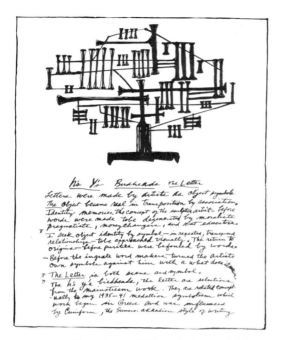

Page from a Willard Gallery exhibition announcement, 1951.

Sketch of *36 Bird Heads,* in a notebook of c. 1950–54.

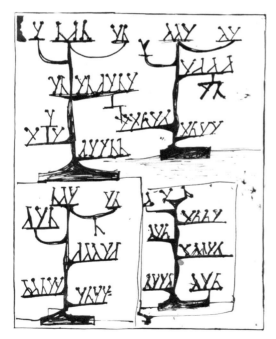

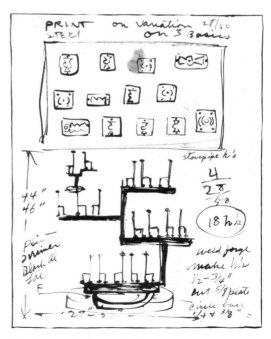

Preliminary sketches for *24 Greek Y's,* in a notebook of c. 1950–54.

Preliminary sketch for *17 h's,* in a notebook of c. 1944–54.

Sketch of *The Fish*, in a notebook of c. 1950–54.

Preliminary sketches for *Cockfight*, in a notebook of c. 1938–45.

Notes for *David Smith Makes a Sculpture*

David Smith wrote these notes for Elaine de Kooning for her article on his work published in Art News, *September, 1951. They were printed intact in* Art News, *January, 1969.*

I follow no set procedure in starting a sculpture. Some works start out as chalk drawings on the cement floor, with cut steel forms working into the drawings. When the structure can become united, it is welded into position upright. Then the added dimension requires different considerations over the more or less profile form of the floor drawing assembly.

Sometimes I make a lot of drawings using possibly one relationship on each drawing which will add up in the final work. Sometimes sculptures just start with no drawing at all. This was the case of *The Fish,** which is some six feet high and about five feet long. My drawings are made either in work books or on large sheets of linen rag. I stock bundles of several types, forgetting the cost so I can be free with it. The cost problem I have to forget on everything, because it is always more than I can afford—more than I get back from sales—most years, more than I earn. My shop is somewhat like the Federal Government, always running with greater expenditures than income and winding up with loans.

For instance, 100 troy ounces of silver solder cost over $100, phoscopper costs $4 a pound, nickel and stainless steel electrodes cost $1.65 to $2 a pound, a sheet of stainless steel ⅛ inch thick, four feet by eight feet costs $83, etc. When I'm involved aesthetically I cannot consider cost, I work by the need of what each material can do. Usually the costly materials do not even show, as their use has been functional.

The traditions for steel do not exist that govern bronze finishes, patinas, or casting limits. There are no preconceived limits established as there are for marble, the aesthetics of grain and surface or the physical limits of mass to strength. Direction by natural grain, hand rubbing, monolithic structure, or the controls of wood do not apply physically or traditionally to steel.

Steel has the greatest tensile strength, the most facile working ability, as long as its nature relates to the aesthetic demand. It can join with its parent metal or other metals varying in colors, or act as a base for metal deposition, paint, or its own natural oxide, [the molecule of] which is only one oxygen atom less than the artistic range of iron oxides.

I have two studios. One clean, one dirty, one warm, one cold. The house studio contains drawing tables, etching press, cabinets for work

* Smith later did at least one sketch of *The Fish:* see page 72.

records, photos, and drawing paper stock. The shop is a cinderblock structure, transite roofed, and has a full row of north window skylights set at a 30 degree angle. With heat in each end it is usable to zero weather.

I do not resent the cost of the best material or the finest tools and equipment. Every labor-saving machine, every safety device I can afford I consider necessary. Stocks of bolts, nuts, taps, dies, paints, solvents, acids, protective coatings, oils, grinding wheels, polishing discs, dry pigments, waxes, chemicals, spare machine parts, are kept stocked on steel shelving, more or less patterned after a factory stockroom.

Stainless steel, bronze, copper, aluminum are stocked in ⅛ inch by 4 foot by 8 foot sheets for fabricating. Cold and hot rolled 4 foot by 8 foot sheets are stacked outside the shop in thicknesses from ⅛ inch to ⅞ inch. Lengths of strips, shapes, and bar stock are racked in the basement of the house or interlaced in the joists of the roof. Maybe I brag a bit about my stock, but it is larger since I've been on a Guggenheim Fellowship than it ever has been before. I mention this not because it has anything to do with art, but it indicates how important it is to have material on hand, that the aesthetic vision is not limited by material need, which has been the case too much of my life.

By the amount of work I produce it must be evident that the most functional tools must be used. I've no aesthetic interest in tool marks; my aim in material function is the same as in locomotive building, to arrive at a given functional form in the most efficient manner. The locomotive method bows to no accepted theory in fabrication. It stands upon the merit of the finished product. The locomotive function incorporates castings, forgings, rivets, welding, brazing, bolts, screws, shrink fits, all used because of their respective efficiency in arriving at a functioning object. Each method imparts its function to varying materials. I use the same method in organizing the visual aesthetic end. I make no claim for my work method over other mediums. I do not use it to the exclusion of other mediums. A certain feeling for form will develop with technical skill, but imaginative form (viz. aesthetic vision) is not a guarantee for high technique.

I handle my machines and materials with ease—their physical resistance and the noise they make in use do not interfere with my thinking and aesthetic flow. The change of one machine or tool to the other means no more than changing brushes to a painter or chisels to a carver.

I do not accept the monolithic limit in the tradition of sculpture. Sculpture is as free as the mind, as complex as life, its statement as full as the other visual mediums combined. I identify form in relationship to man. The front view of a person is ofttimes complete in statement. Sculpture to me may be 1-2-3-4 sides and top view since the bottom by law is the base. Projection of indicated form, continuance of an uncompleted side I leave to the viewer or the suggestion of a solid by lines, or the vision of the forms revolving at given or varying speeds. All such possibilities I consider and expect the viewer to contemplate.

When such incompletions are evident, usually there are directives which can enable the viewer to complete the concept with the given form. The art form should not be platitudinous, predigested, with no intellectual or emotional demands on the consumer.

When I make sculpture all the speeds, projections, gyrations, light changes are involved in my vision, as such things I know in movement associate with all the possibilities possible in other relationships. Possibly steel is so beautiful because of all the movement associated with it, its strength and function. Yet it is also brutal, the rapist, the murderer, and death-dealing giants are also its offspring. But in my Spectre series, I speak of these things and it seems most functional in its method of statement.

Since 1936 I have modeled wax for single bronze castings. I have carved marble and wood, but the major number of works have been steel, which is my most fluent medium and which I control from start to completed work without interruption. There is gratification of being both conceiver and executor without intrusion. A sculpture is not quickly produced; it takes time, during which time the conviction must be deep and lasting. Michelangelo spoke about noise and marble dust in our profession, but I finish the day more like a greaseball than a miller. But my concepts still would not permit me to trade it for cleaner pursuits.

Distance within the work is not an illusion, it relates to the known measure known as inches in most of our considerations. Inches are rather big, monotonous chunks related to big flat feet. The only even inch relationship will be found in the sculpture base wherein the units 4-6-8-12, etc., are used in mechanical support. Rarely will an even inch be involved in visual space, and when it is approached it will occur plus or minus in variants of odd thousandths, odd 64ths, 32nds, and 16ths. This is not planned consciously. It is not important, but is my natural reaction to symbolic life. Unit relationships within a work usually involve the number 7 or a division of its parts. I wasn't conscious of this until I looked back, but the natural selection seems influenced by art mythology.

My work day begins at 10 or 11 A.M. after a leisurely breakfast and an hour of reading. The shop is 800 feet from the house. I carry my 2 P.M. lunch and return to the house at 7 for dinner. The work day ends from 1 to 2 A.M. with time out for coffee at 11:30. My shop here is called the Terminal Iron Works, since it closer defines my beginning and my method than to call it "studio."

At 11:30 when I have evening coffee and listen to WQXR on AM, I never fail to think of the Terminal Iron Works at 1 Atlantic Avenue, Brooklyn, and the coffeepot nearby where I went, same time, same station. The iron works in Brooklyn was surrounded by all-night activity—ships loading, barges refueling, ferries tied up at the dock. It was awake 24 hours a day, harbor activity in front, truck transports on Furman Street behind. In contrast the mountains are quiet except for occasional animal noises. Sometimes Streevers's hounds run foxes all night and I can hear them baying as I close up shop. Rarely does a car pass at night. There is no habitation between our road and the Schroon River four miles cross country. I enjoy the phenomenon of nature, the sounds, the Northern Lights, stars, animal calls, as I did the harbor lights, tugboat whistles, buoy clanks, the yelling of men on barges around the T.I.W. in Brooklyn. I sit up here and dream of the city as I used to dream of the mountains when I sat on the dock in Brooklyn.

I like my solitude, black coffee, and daydreams. I like the changes of nature; no two days or nights are the same. In Brooklyn what was nature was all manmade and mechanical, but I like both. I like the companionship of music, I sometimes can get WNYC but always WQXR, Montreal, Vancouver, or Toronto. I use the music as company in the manual labor part of sculpture, of which there is much. The work flow of energy demanded by sculpture wherein mental exhaustion is accompanied by physical exhaustion provides the only balance I've ever found, and as far as I know is the only way of life.

Of course I get rides on. When I'm working I get so wound up with work that sleep doesn't come and I work through to 3-4-5 in the morning. This I did back in Brooklyn. All my life the work day has been any part of the 24, on oil tankers, driving hacks, going to school, all three shifts in factories. I once worked in a bank, but cannot stand the routine life. Any two-thirds of the 24 hours are wonderful as long as I can choose.

After 1 A.M. certain routine work has to be done, clearing up, repairing machines, oiling, painting, etc. I tune in WOR and listen to Nick's, Café Society, Eddie Condon's, whoever is on. After several months of good work, when I feel I deserve a reward, I go to New York, concerts at YMHA, gallery shows, museums, eat seafood, Chinese, go to Eddie's, Nick's, Sixth Avenue Cafeteria, Artists Club, Cedar Tavern, run into up-late artists, bum around chewing the fat, talk shop, finish up eating breakfast on Eighth Street, and ride it as hard and as long as I can for a few days, then back to the hills.

Sculpture is a problem. Both to me and to my dealer, the Willard Gallery. Aside from sales, the problem of transport and storage is immense. The intrinsic cost ofttimes is half its price, and never less than

David Smith

one-third. Only a few serious dealers handle it; some museums and a few collectors buy it. As dwelling space contracts, the size and concept of sculpture increases. I foresee no particular use, other than aesthetic, in society, least of all architecture. But demand was never the thing that made art in our period of civilization.

Sometimes I work on two and possibly four pieces at one time, conceptually involved on one, conceptually in abeyance on another waiting for relationships to complete; and on one or two others finished but for a casting to come from the foundry or grinding, finishing and a few hours of manual labor waiting to be done. Sometimes it's only a matter of mounting, weighing, measuring, and naming. Such detail work fits in schedule when the muse has gone. I maintain my identity by regular work, there is always labor when inspiration has fled, but inspiration returns quicker when identity and the work stream are maintained. Actually time overtakes much of my projects. I get only half of my vision into material form. The rest remains as drawings, which, after a certain time growth, I cannot return to because the pressing demand is the future. I have no organized procedure in creating. *The Fish* went through from start to finish with a small drawing in my work book, during its middle stage. *The Cathedral* matured from start to finish with no drawings. Usually there are drawings, anything from sketches in pocket notebooks to dozens of big sheet paintings.

Perception and Reality

This speech, given at Williams College on December 17, 1951, is one of several variations on the same theme presented by Smith during the early 1950's.

I wish to remind you of the hypocritical world that art enters. One Pulitzer Prize poet stated that "vitamins and profits alone are not worth dying for. . . . The republic was founded and preserved by men and women who frankly acknowledged themselves dependent on God." I find poet [Robert] Hillyer a dreamer. I find such noble concepts to be the pretense of our people with their practice nowhere near the pretense, as in the case of most stated American glories: freedom, equality, the ten commandments, the bill of rights. Belief is belied by compromise and contradiction in behavior.

The bastardization which materialistic enterprise has inflicted upon both culture and spiritual response by its control of communication media is all too evident. Truth, as it relates to the republic and its democratically elected officials, is a *qualified theorem* in the eyes of the average man. The poetic use of words has been ruined by commercials. *That one hour* in a hundred on the radio when classical music is presented is cut and graded for the purpose of softening the audience preparatory to the commercial, a mollifying delivery of quarter truths. The type of classical music played is important here; it must be familiar, and, as Virgil Thomson has pointed out, one of a standard repertoire of fifty symphonies. A contemporary classic such as a Schönberg composition is not a safe or suitable introduction to a soothing commercial. Hence the value and necessity of universally accepted symphony music to the world of sponsors, whose choice ultimately sets the limits to what is called in the trade, our listening pleasure.

It is no wonder that when the artist speaks with what he calls truth, the audience, accustomed to censored digests and synthetic catharsis, views it as a foreign language. Art divorced from commercial persuasion, having little dollars-and-cents value, is regarded with suspicion.

People wanting to be told something, *given the last word,* will not find it in art. Art is not didactic. It is not final; it is always waiting for the projection of the viewer's perceptive powers. Even from the creator's position, the work represents a segment of his life, based on the history of his previous works, awaiting the continuity of the works to follow. In a sense a work of art is never finished.

My concept as an artist is a revolt against the well-worn beauties in the form of a statue. Rather I would prefer my assemblages to be the savage idols of basic patterns, the veiled directives, subconscious associations, *the image recall* of orders more true than the object itself, resulting in vision, in aura, rather than object reality.

No two people see the same work of art because no two people are each other. No two people see the same apple or pear, because a pear is not a pear except in theory. When seen, a pear is an image. It is red, green, hard, soft, juicy, rotten, falling, rolling, segmented, sweet, sour, sensuously felt. A pear is a violin, a pear is a woman's hips. Pear and violin have strings, woman has hair. Pear and woman have seeds, violin has notes, soft violin, hard woman, sour notes—associations can go on indefinitely only to show that a fruit can only exist as an eidetic image because it cannot exist in reality without associations.

If a painter paints a pear, the beholder's mind can select and experience the desired action in a flash. The depth of association, hence the completeness of the image in this recognition flash, is dependent upon the will of the beholder. The response to pear varies greatly, depending upon what comes through after censoring, and so it is with the response to art. Neither perception of pear nor perception of a painting requires

David Smith

faculties beyond those of an average man. Perception through vision is a highly accelerated response, so fast, so complex, so free that it cannot be pinned down by the very recent limited science of word communication. To understand a work of art, it must be seen and perceived, not worded. Words can be used to place art historically, to set it in social context, to describe the movements, to relate it to other works, to state individual preferences, and to set the scene all around it. But the actual understanding of a work of art only comes through the process by which it was created—and that was by perception.

The Language Is Image

The words I use in talking about art do not bear close relationship to making art, nor are they necessary directives or useful explanations. They may represent views that govern some choice in sublimation—censored exchange or as opposites. When I work the train of thought has no words, it is simply all in the visual world, the language is image. If I write it is not at the expense of my work, it is done during travel and non-work pursuit.

Probably I resent the word world (Joyce, etc., excepted) because it has become the tool of pragmatists, has shown limited change, has rejected creative extension. It seems that the pragmatists have turned words against their creators when dealing with perception. Most of the words on art have been an actual hindrance to the understanding of art perception. This anti-art verbiage starts in elementary grades and is constant throughout the majority of educational institutions, both state and sectarian.

Judging from cuneiform, Chinese and other ancient texts, the object symbols formed identities upon which letters and words were later developed. Their business and exploitation use has become dominant over their poetic-communicative use, which explains one facet of their inadequateness.

Thirty or forty thousand years ago primitive man did not have the word picture, nor this demand for limited vision. His relationship to the object was with all its parts and function, by selection, or the eidetic image.

Since recorded origins true perception in art has had various official safeguards and mono-interpretations, such limits in making art or receiv-

From *Arts and Architecture*, February, 1952.

ing art being more or less law and answering to one interpretation, usually literary or confined to an official symbol language for religio-commercial use.

The cave man from Altamira to Rhodesia had produced true reality by the eidetic image. This image even today defies word explanation as does any art, since it is simply to be received by a totally different physical sense.

The true reality of an apple is not any one naturalistic image. The eye of man is not a camera eye, it is a cerebral eye. It is not a two-dimensional photograph, nor any one view. The reality is actually all apples in all actions. Apples are red, yellow, green, round, halved, quartered, sweet, sour, rotten, sensuously felt, hanging, crushed to juice, and all the associations two years would take to tabulate, yet when stimulated the mind can select and experience the desired action in a flash; "apple" is meaningless without memory.

Perception through vision is a highly accelerated response, so fast, so complex, so free that these qualities are unattainable by the very recent limited science of word communication.

In perceiving, all men are potentially equal. The mind records everything the senses experience. No man has sensed anything another has not, or lacks the components and power to assemble. The word version of art represents both censoring and prejudice. Yet it is the version educational institutions advocate and is the general public's basic response. Yet perception open to any man, in any status, ignores the language barrier.

My realities giving impetus to a work which is a train of hooked visions arise from very ordinary locales—the arrangement of things under an old board; stress patterns; fissures; the structure pattern of growth; stains; tracks of men, animals, machines; the accidental or unknown order of forces; accidental evidences such as spilled paint, patched sidewalks, broken parts, structural faults; the force lines in rock or marble laid by glacial sedimentation. Realistic all, made by ancient pattern or unknown force to be recorded, repeated, varied, transformed in analogy or as keys to contemporary celebrations. Some works are the celebration of wonders. After several of these a specter. In my life, joy, peace are always menaced. Survival, not only from commercial destruction but the threat of daily existence, the battle of money for material—and welfare during.

I date my aesthetic heritage from Impressionism. Since Impressionism, the realities from which art has come have all been the properties of ordinary man; the still life has been from the working man's household; the characters, environment, landscape have been of common nature. The bourgeois or upper-class reality and grandeur pretension

David Smith

have not been the realities which the artist's eyes have transformed. The controls of my art are not outside the daily vision of common man. The vision and organization are very personal and, I hope, my own.

The hostile demand for reality usually is the stopped image, which to me has no place in art, being a totally different value from perception and one related more to photography than art. Hostility to art often exists as a fear of a misunderstood intellectualism.

Primitive man attained the eidetic image. This must have been attained by great desire and affection. At least it was not hostility based on historic standards or censored by self-consciousness.

Limits and lack may exist in the artist's sense-presentation. Some artists produce for greater sense-perception. Perception is a quality which all men exercise, there being a difference in degree. The creation of known forms or symbols, related or associated into a new image not existing before, does not exclude it from understanding; since it comes from common subconscious registry, nothing is secret or mystical.

For instance, the sculpture called *Hudson River Landscape* came in part from drawings made on a train between Albany and Poughkeepsie. A synthesis of drawings from ten trips over a seventy-five mile stretch; yet later when I shook a quart bottle of India ink it flew over my hand, it looked like my landscape. I placed my hand on paper—from the image left I traveled with the landscape to other landscapes and their objects —with additions, deductions, directives which flashed past too fast to tabulate but elements of which are in the sculpture. Is *Hudson River Landscape* the Hudson River or is it the travel, the vision; or does it matter? The sculpture exists on its own, it is an entity. The name is an affectionate designation of the point prior to the travel. My object was not these words or the Hudson River but the existence of the sculpture. Your response may not travel down the Hudson River, but it may travel on any river or on a higher level, travel through form-response by choice known better by your own recall. I have intensified only part of the related clues; the sculpture possesses nothing unknown to you. I want you to travel, by perception, the path I traveled in creating it.

You can reject it, like it, pretend to like it, or almost like it, but its understanding will never come with words, which had no part in its making, nor can they truly explain the wonders of the human sensorium.

The New Sculpture

A symposium on "The New Sculpture," held at the Museum of Modern Art on February 21, 1952, included this paper by David Smith.

Before knowing what art was or before going to art school, as a factory worker I was acquainted with steel and the machines used in forging it. During my second year in art school I learned about Cubism, Picasso, and González through *Cahiers d'Art*. From them I learned that art was being made with steel—the material and machines that had previously meant only labor and earning power.

While my technical liberation came from Picasso's friend and countryman González, my aesthetics were more influenced by Kandinsky, Mondrian, and Cubism. My student period was only involved with painting. The painting developed into raised levels from the canvas. Gradually the canvas became the base, and the painting was a sculpture. I have never recognized any separation except one element of dimension. The first painting of cave man was both carved line and color, a natural reaction and a total statement.

My first steel sculpture was made in the summer of 1933, with borrowed equipment. The same year I started to accumulate equipment and moved into the Terminal Iron Works on the Brooklyn waterfront. My work of 1934–36 was often referred to as line sculpture, but to me it was as complete a statement about form and color as I could make. The majority of work in my first show at the East River Gallery in 1938 was painted. I do not recognize the limits where painting ends and sculpture begins.

Since the turn of the century painters have led the aesthetic front both in number and in concept. Outside of Brancusi, the greatest sculptures were made by painters. Sculpture is more immediate than painting for visual action. Natural constants such as gravity, space, and hard objects are the physicals of the sculpture process. Consequently they flow more freely into the act of vision than the illusion of constants used in painting. The fact that these constants or premises need no translation should make sculpture the medium of greatest vision. This I mention as a theoretic possibility; but the concept of the resistance of material is an element which is unique to this art form. A sculpture is a thing, an object. A painting is an illusion. There is a difference in degree in actual space and the absolute difference in gravity.

My position for vision in my works aims to be in it, and not a scientific physical viewing it as subject. I wish to comment in the travel. It

David Smith

is an adventure viewed. I do not enter its order as lover, brother or associate, I seem to view it equally as from the traveling height of a plane two miles up, or from my mountain workshop viewing a cloud-like procession.

In the Reisho school of Chinese character writing, the graphic aim was to show the force of carving in stone or engraving in steel. It is easy to see how this noble intent could express with such conviction. A Chinese painter explained that although the long blade leaves of an orchid droop toward the earth, they all long to point to the sky. This Chinese attitude of cloud-longing is an eye through which I view form in works of celebration and, conversely, in those of a specter nature.

Certain Japanese formalities seem close to me, such as the beginning of a stroke outside the paper continuing through the drawing space to project beyond, so that the included part possesses both the power of origin and projection. This produces the impression of strength, and if drops fall they become attributes or relationships. Similarly, if the brush flows dry into hair marks, such may be greater in energy, having at least a natural quality not to be reworked, being sufficient in intent to convey the stronger content. It is not Japanese painting but some of the principles involved that have meaning to me. Another Japanese concept demands that when representing an object suggesting strength—like rocks, talons, claws, tree branches—the moment the brush is applied the sentiment of strength must be invoked and felt through the artist's system, and so transmitted into the object painted. And that this nervous current must be continuous and of equal intensity while the work proceeds. As my material already possesses strength akin to the Japanese power-stroke intent, I take delight in using steel as a fluid with which to fashion velvet form within images when the intensity and feeling are the forces within the concept.

I have never planned a work of art to be left in the semi-finished state, or in the material not meant to be final. The intermediate stage of pattern, with the casting unrealized, would leave me in suspense. Rather I am content to leave hundreds of sculptures in drawings which time, cost, and conceptual change have passed by. Even with my production, some twenty works a year, production costs force limits in scale, material, and output, but if I depended on plaster and wax for bronze casting, the number of works would be cut in half.

When mass space is indicated by line or fenced form, the work time demanded due to the resistance of material before unity, the suspension and projection required by the natural law of gravity, demand more pre-meditation and sustained conviction than when the same form is drawn on a planar surface. The line contour with its variations and its comment on mass space is more acute than bulk shape. In vision the overlay of shapes seen through each other not only permits each shape to retain its individual intent but in juxtaposition highly multiplies the associations of the new and more complex unity.

I do not work with a conscious and specific conviction about a piece of sculpture. Such a decision is not an aim. The works you see are segments of my work life. If you prefer one work over another, it is your privilege, but it does not interest me. The work is a statement of identity, it comes from a stream, it is related to my past works, the three or four works in process and the work yet to come. I will accept your rejection, but I will not consider your criticism any more than I will concerning my life.

I do not consciously feel revolt against past art or European art in particular. I am conscious of the security of that development, from world art and contemporary technics, which permit my particular existence to be active in its own right with its own direction. This is not an exclusive position. This feeling is in part accountable for the tremendous art surge which exists throughout the country. And more so here than in any part of the world.

The material called iron or steel I hold in high respect. What it can do in arriving at a form economically, no other material can do. The metal itself possesses little art history. What associations it possesses are those of this century: power, structure, movement, progress, suspension, destruction, brutality. The method of unifying parts to completion need not be evident, especially if craft evidence distracts from the conceptual end. Yet the need to observe the virtue of the material, its natural planes, its hard lines, its natural oxides, its need for paint or its unifying method is only valid when within concept. These points related to the steel concept are minor and depend wholly upon the conceptual realization of the sculptor, but they are unique and have never existed before this century.

In work progress, I control the entire process from origin to finish. There are no in-between craftsmen or process distortions. It is the complete and total processing of the work of art. Economically this process has high virtue over other metal means. Outside of aesthetic considerations, the labor costs in casting are higher than the sculptor's own wages. Direct work is not meant to replace casting, but it more often conforms to my concept. But casting is a method and concept which holds its function as it has for 6,000 years.

The accommodation to each particular machine tool and its method is made familiar by use. The construction of the whole from its parts is made by fairly unconscious change of machine tools. The machine tool becomes an instrument of aesthetics in the art of addition. The transfor-

David Smith

mation of unit parts into a unified whole from seemingly disparate units, by repeated action, result in full order. In fact, my beginning before I knew about art had already been conditioned to the machine—the part of the whole, by addition, or the quantity into quality concept. This aesthetic process relates closer to the mode of painting than to the historic making of sculpture.

The term "vulgar" is a quality, the extreme to which I want to project form, and it may be society's vulgarity, but it is my beauty. The celebrations, the poetic statement in the form of cloud-longing is always menaced by brutality. The cloud-fearing of specters has always the note of hope, and within the vulgarity of the form an upturn of beauty. Despite the subject of brutality, the application must show love. The rape of man by war machine will show the poetic use of form in its making. The beauties of nature do not conceal destruction and degeneration. Form will flower with spikes of steel, the savage idols of basic patterns. The point of departure will start at departure. The metaphor will be the metaphor of a metaphor, and then totally oppose it.

I believe only artists truly understand art, because art is best understood by following the visionary path of the creator who produces it. The Philistines will not attempt the projection. A work of art is produced by an expert. There must be expertness in its perception. There are degrees in expertness—some come close, some are on the fringe, some pretend. Degrees of expertness naturally apply to both the artists creating and the audience response.

Atmosphere of the Early Thirties

The following notes on the 1930's are from a note- and sketchbook kept about 1952.

One did not feel disowned—only ignored and much alone, with a vague pressure from authority that art couldn't be made here. It was a time of temporary expatriates, not that they made art more in France but that they talked it, and when here were happier there; and not that their concept was more avant than ours but they were under its shadow there and we were in the windy openness here. Ideas were sought as the end but the result often registered in purely performance. Being far away, depending upon *Cahiers d'Art* and the return of patriots often left us trying for the details instead of the whole. I remember watching a painter,

Gorky, work over an area edge probably a hundred times to reach an infinite without changing the rest of the picture, following Graham's recount of the import put in Paris on the "edge of paint." We all grasped on everything new, and despite the atmosphere of New York worked on everything but our own identities. I make exceptions for Graham and Davis, especially Davis, who though at his least recognized or exhibited stage was the solid citizen for a group a bit younger who were trying to find their stride. Matulka had a small school on Fourteenth Street but maintained a rather secluded seriousness painting away on Eighty-ninth Street East, as he still does. [Joseph] Stella often was around Romany Marie's but I did not think his work matched the monopoly discourse he preferred. Xceron was back and forth between Paris and New York, and in Paris wrote art criticism for several American papers.

Our hangouts were Stewart's Cafeteria on Seventh Avenue near Fourteenth Street close to Davis's studio and school, and 5¢ coffee was much closer to our standards, but on occasion we went to the Dutchman's, McSorley's and Romany Marie's. We followed Romany Marie from Eighth Street, where Gorky once gave a chalk talk on Cubism, to several other locations. Her place came closer to being a Continental café with its varied types of professionals than any other place I knew. It was in Marie's where we once formed a group, Graham, Edgar Levy, Resnikoff, de Kooning, Gorky and myself with Davis being asked to join. This was short-lived. We never exhibited and we lasted in union about thirty days. Our only action was to notify the Whitney Museum that we were a group and would only exhibit in the 1935 abstract show if all were asked. Some of us were, some exhibited, some didn't, and that ended our group. But we were all what was then termed abstractionists.

The Sculptor and His Problems

The following is a speech given at the Woodstock Conference of Artists, Woodstock, New York, August 23, 1952.

To the creative artist it is doubtful if aesthetics have any value except as literature. It is doubtful if they have any value to his historic understanding of art, because his aesthetics are a totality of visual memories of art images and not words. Even when aesthetics exist in his time, relating to his work, they are made after the work of art is completed, by minds and language other than the artist's. Historically, he is not subject to what a pedant thinks another artist thought, when he has direct communication with artists of all ages, in their own language.

Aesthetic qualities of the artist's work are in a sense a projection into the future, compared to verbal aesthetics which are based upon the past.

From the aesthetic point of view, at the time of creation, the work of art deals with vulgarization. The work of art does not change. The mellowing of time, the pedant's talk, only legitimize it in the minds of the audience who wish to hear but refuse to see.

Aesthetics have value for those who do not like art but who are willing to talk about it.

The creative artist should not be impressed by the written directives, for his are intuitive and emotional. To make art, the artist must deal with unconscious controls, controls which have no echo but which guide him, direct and first-hand.

The artist does not deny aesthetics, but his aesthetics are memory retentions visually selected, carry no moral, and do not operate within word limits. Verbally stated aesthetic summations are of no benefit in the making of a work of art. Generally considered, aesthetics in verbal form are a bastardization of the creative artist's beauties. They represent a craft or trade alien to creating.

Aesthetics have been the limit which lesser minds hold as rules to keep the creative artist inside the verbal realm and away from his visual world. Actually philosophy of art and the history of art have nothing to do with the creative artist's point of view. They are entirely different fields. But the layman is apt to become confused if he isn't able to make this differentiation. He often expects the artist to perform according to the philosopher's truth theorems or the historian's generalities.

The stingy logic of the philosopher, his suspicion that the irrational creative menaces the will, excludes that all-important element of art-making which I will call affection. This feeling of affection which dominates art-making has nothing to do with the philosopher's need for rationalization.

The arguments pro and con have already been taken by Chairman [George] Boas, and I am convinced that he is an aesthetician with affinity toward the artist, with an understanding of the contemporary point of view. Since all the questions have been handled in an extremely rational manner, there is no point in continuing the conference except to handle what is irrational, or what the aestheticians call irrational.

When you ask the question to black—is it white? Is it day or night, good or evil, positive or negative? Is it life or death? Is it the superficial scientific explanation about the absence of light? Is it a solid wall or is it space? Is it paint, a man, a father? Or does it come out blank having been censored out by some unknown or unrecognizable association?

There is no one answer. Black is no one thing. The answer depends upon impression. The importance of what black means depends upon your conviction and your artistic projection of black; depends upon your poetic vision, your mythopoetic view, your myth of black. And to the creative mind the dream and myth of black is more the truth of black than the scientific theory or the dictionary explanation or the philosopher's account of black. Black is an article of vision defying translation and semantics.

Aesthetics, the Artist, and the Audience

The following speech was given at Deerfield, Massachusetts, on September 24, 1952.

I wish to present my conclusions first and start my presentation backward.

Time is a new dimension in sculpture, and since I don't accent bulk-mass and prefer open delineation and transparent form—so that the front views through to the back—the same method by statement may work as well.

To the creative artist, in the making of art it is doubtful whether aesthetics have any value to him.

The truly creative artist deals with vulgarity.

Nobody understands art but the artist.

Affection for art is the sole property of the artist. The majority approach art with hostility.

The artist deserves to be belligerent to the majority.

The artist is a product of his time, and his belligerence is a defense and not a preference.

There is no such thing as a layman. The layman is either an art lover or an art rejector.

The viewer of art, the art lover, has the privilege of accepting or rejecting. But there is no such thing as a layman. He is either a pretender or the verbalizer.

Masterpieces are made today.

Aesthetics are written conclusions or directives. The creative artist should not be impressed by verbal directives. His aesthetics are primarily unconscious and of a visual recording. No words or summations are involved. The artist does not deny aesthetics or the history of art. The myth in art, the history of art, are both enjoyed and used, but they

1. *Bay Rum Dock, St. Thomas,* c. 1932. Medium and dimensions unknown. Private collection. Photograph by David Smith.

2. Collage, c. 1931. Medium and dimensions unknown. Private collection. Photograph by David Smith.

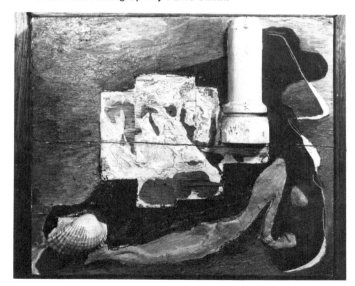

3. Untitled, 1933. Coral, wood, 5⅝ x 5⅛ x 6⅜ inches. Estate of the artist. Photograph by David Smith.

4. Field at Bolton Landing, c. 1932. Photograph by David Smith.

5. Dorothy Dehner at Bolton Landing, 1932. Photograph by David Smith.

6. View of the Smith's Bolton Landing farmhouse, taken from the construction site of the new shop, c. 1940.

7. Dorothy Dehner and David Smith embarking for Europe in October,
    1935.

8. David Smith at the Brooklyn Terminal Iron Works, c. 1937. *Construction
    in Bent Planes,* 1936 (upper left). *Sculptor and Model,* 1937 (upper right).
    Unidentified sculpture (lower left). *Bent Blade Plane,* 1936 (lower right).

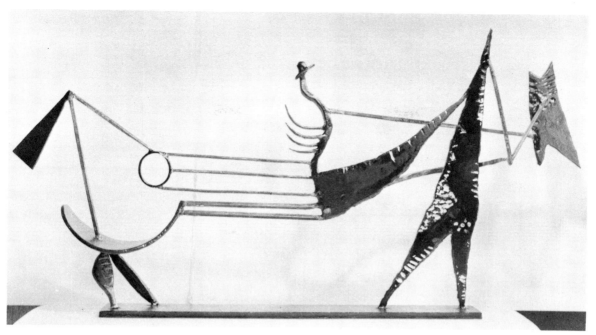

9. *Horse and Rider (Horseman),* 1937. WPA work, medium, dimensions, and whereabouts unknown. From the New York Federal Art Project records in the Archives of American Art, Smithsonian Institution, Washington, D.C. Photograph by Bratter.

10. Page from a notebook of c. 1944–54.

11. *Balsa Wood Construction,* 1938. WPA work, medium, dimensions, and whereabouts unknown. From the New York Federal Art Project records in the Archives of American Art, Smithsonian Institution, Washington, D.C. Photograph by Bratter.

12. Preliminary sketches for *Balsa Wood Construction,* in a notebook of c. 1938–45.

13. *Headscrew,* 1939 (left). Wrought iron, 13¼ x 17¼ x 4 inches. Whereabouts unknown. *Growing Forms,* 1939 (right). Cast aluminum, 28 x 9 x 6 inches. Two casts known: Collection Charles E. Palmer; Estate of the artist. Photograph by Andreas Feininger.

14. *Structure of Arches,* 1939 (left). Steel with cadmium and copper plating, 39 x 48 x 30 inches. Collection Mrs. Douglass Crockwell. *Vertical Structure,* 1939 (right). Steel with copper, 45⅞ x 33½ x 28⅜ inches. Estate of the artist. Photograph by David Smith.

(above)

15. *Medal for Dishonor No. 9—Bombing Civilian Populations,* 1939. Plaster model for master bronze, 10 inches in diameter. Estate of the artist. Photograph by David Smith.

(right)

16. Page from a medical book belonging to John Graham, photographed by David Smith in the 1930's.

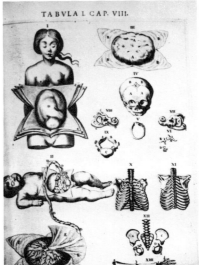

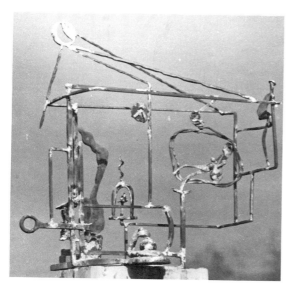

17. *Interior for Exterior,* 1939. Steel, bronze, 18 x 22 x 23¼ inches. Collection Mr. and Mrs. Orin M. Raphael. Photograph by David Smith.

18. *Ad Mare,* 1939. Steel, 30 x 28 x 9 inches. Collection Mrs. Sibley Smith. Photograph by David Smith.

19. *Bathers,* 1940. Steel, 14 inches high x 14 inches wide. Collection Marian Willard Johnson. Photograph by David Smith.

20. *Agricola Head,* 1933 (left). Iron, steel painted red, 18⅜ x 10⅛ x 7¾ inches. *Chain Head,* 1933 (center). Iron, 18½ x 12 x 9 inches. *Saw Head,* 1933 (right). Iron painted orange, bronze, 17 x 11¼ x 8¼ inches. Estate of the artist. Photograph by David Smith.

21. *War Spectre,* 1944. Steel painted black, 11¼ x 22 x 6 inches. Collection Mr. and Mrs. Jan de Graaff. Photograph by David Smith.

23. Preliminary sketch for *Woman Music,* in a
notebook of c. 1942.

22. *Woman Music,* 1944. Steel painted ocher, 18
inches high x 9 inches wide. Collection Victor
Wolfson. Photograph by David Smith.

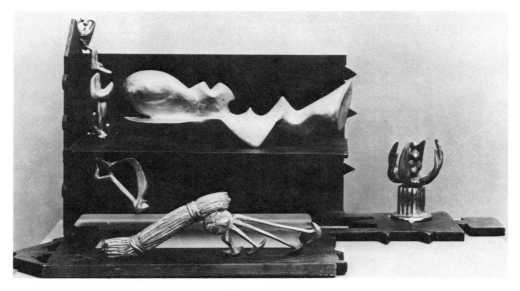

24. *Reliquary House,* 1945. Bronze, steel painted black, 12½ x 25½ x 11¾ inches. Collection
Mr. and Mrs. David Mirvish. Photograph by David Smith.

25. Preliminary sketches for *Reliquary House,* in a notebook of c. 1938–45.

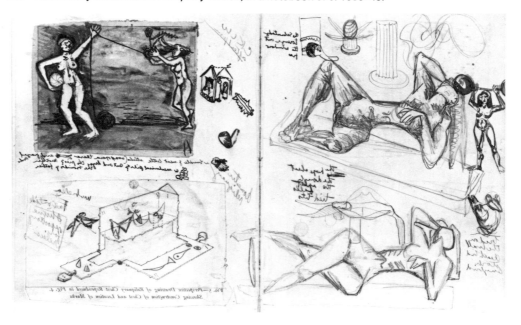

(above left)

26. *Pillar of Sunday,* 1945. Steel painted pink, 30½ x 18 x 9½ inches. Indiana University Art Museum, Bloomington. Photograph by David Smith.

(above right)

27. *Cockfight,* 1945. Steel, 45½ inches high. The St. Louis Museum, St. Louis, Missouri. Photograph by David Smith.

(right)

28. *False Peace Spectre,* 1945. Bronze, steel painted blue, 12½ x 27¼ x 10¾ inches. Private collection. Photograph by David Smith.

29. *House in a Landscape (Rural Landscape with Manless House),* 1945. Steel, 18½ x 24¾ x 6 inches. Collection George M. Irwin. Photograph by David Smith.

30. *Spectre Riding the Golden Ass,* 1945. Bronze, 11¾ x 12¼ x 4 inches. The Detroit Institute of Arts, Detroit, Michigan; Gift of Robert H. Tannahil. Photograph by David Smith.

32. *Home of the Welder,* 1945. Steel, 21 x 17⅜ x 14 inches. Estate of the artist. Photograph by David Smith.

31. *Tahstvaat,* 1946. Steel, cast iron, 28¼ x 13¾ x 10⅝ inches. The University of Michigan Museum of Art, Ann Arbor. Photograph by David Smith.

33. *Blackburn, Song of an Irish Blacksmith,* 1949–50. Steel, bronze, 46¼ x 40¾ x 24 inches. Wilhelm Lehmbruck Museum, Duisberg, Germany. Photograph by David Smith.

are utilized by the memory of vision which is the only language in which the artist who made the work of art intended it to be understood.

I have spoken of the artist's use of the vulgar. But this term I use because, to the professional aesthetician, it is a vulgarity in his code of beauty, because he has not recognized it as yet or made rules for its acceptance. To the creative artist it is his beauty, but to the audience, who will wait for the aesthetician's explanation, it is too new and has not yet hammered its way into acceptance. It will not conform to the past, it is beyond the pale. Art aestheticians can only make conclusions or discourse after the work of art is made. The birth of the idea, the concept, is the important act in the work of art.

Nobody understands art but the artist because nobody is as interested in art, its pursuit, its making, as the artist. This need eliminate no one from enjoying any art—if they do not limit it with preconceived notions of what art should be or demand confinement in which it should stay. The true way to understand the work of art is to travel the path by visual response, similar to the method the artist used in arriving at the work.

Does the onlooker realize the amount of affection which goes into a work of art—the intense affection—belligerent vitality—and total conviction? To the artist it must be total to provide satisfaction. Does the critic, the audience, the philosopher even possess the intensity of affection for the work which its creator possessed? Can they project or understand this belligerent vitality and affection which contemporary art possesses? Or do they deal in the quality at all? Is this emotion too highly keyed—is it outside their lives? Or are they too skeptical? Or do they need written confirmation and general acceptance before they will let their own natural response be admitted to themselves?

All the artists I know find survival and the right to work by means other than the sale of their work. Their work speaks solely by their own conviction. They are not beholden to tradition or directives other than their own. Any artist must meet the world with his work. When he meets the world, what is his aim? Is there a need for aim, if the inner convictions and drive are so great that he will not settle for anything short of the fact that being an artist—and to exercise his mode of expression—is the most important pursuit in the world?

Since the artist cannot exist outside his time, certain social pressure has affected him, certain critical opinion has directed him. He feels the majority rejection, so for whom does he make art? For himself first, for the opinion of other artists next, and specifically those artists in his own mores and in his own aesthetic realm. But his world and his realm is the same world that all others inhabit. He has no secret code or key, no special foresight, environment, brilliance, erudition. He exercises the right of vision—projection—by his own choice. His preference is to be a working and recognized member of his culture, and to have his work accepted.

I have concluded that there is no such thing as a layman, and I believe that because nothing the artist can see or imagine is outside the world of any other man of good will. The professional layman I do not believe is a lover of art. I think he demands verbal explanation in lieu of using his vision. In my category he seeks cover under the layman term to make rejection, because he really wants the word statement where he feels his challenge is on safer ground. Possibly he fears the social stigma of rejecting a work of art. There is no onus upon rejection. That is always the viewer's privilege, to accept or reject a work of art, a school of art, a period of art, but let us keep it clear and not substitute words for art. Our educational system and many of our influences tend to inhibit the natural response. Commercial pressures stress the mass acceptance of one thing. Certain social mores unofficially endorse certain trends. The individual taste in many things other than art is led to be suspect. The simple human response is often questioned unless it can be rated by word explanation.

Yes, masterpieces are made today. Masterpieces are only works of art that people especially like. The twentieth century has produced very many. Present-day, contemporary America is producing masterpieces —a virile, aggressive, increasing number of painters and sculptors not before produced here. Let us not be intimidated by the pretending authorities who write books and term only this and that Mona Lisa as the only masterpiece. Masterpieces are only especially considered works of art. They occur now and they occurred 30,000 years ago.

The aesthetics of contemporary American art have not been written. The forward movement does not have a name. Its heritage is certainly post-Fauvist, post-Cubist, post-Expressionist, post-purist, post-Constructivist. But there are certain outstanding elements involved. One of the forces is freedom, and a belligerent freedom, to reject the established tradition of the verbal aestheticians, philosophers, and critics; instead to express emotionally and directly with the artist himself as subject, without concession to the classic routine, still life, sex, mono-object and the other historic forms. Possibly this is too free, too defiant, to accept that the soul of man's total belief can be the subject of art. No subject is taboo in art. Why cannot the nature of man himself be the subject? There is no order but the order of man. Yet this is great order. There is not even form, as we traditionally know it. There is no chiaroscuro of solid bodies; now space becomes solid, and solids become transparent. Why should we worry that sculpture isn't chiaroscurally solid? Concept is more important than chiaroscuro. Nothing is really unsolid. Mass is en-

David Smith

ergy, space is energy, space is mass. Whether such things are scientific facts is very, very unimportant. Art is poetic. It is poetically irrational. The irrational is the major force in man's nature. And as such the artist still deals with nature. Neither artist nor audience can deal with concepts that are not nature.

Economic Support of Art in America Today

Following is a talk given at an American Federation of Arts conference held at Corning, New York, October 30, 1953.

The artist has been told by almost everybody what art is, what the artist's function is, most often by people who do not perceive, love or make art, but who nonetheless presume the right, because they are laymen, historians or critics or figure somewhere in the art fringe, to make definition.

These are the decadent critics and aestheticians whose first premise is that art can never be as great as it was in the Renaissance.

Some years ago the demoralizing effect of this viewpoint was to bilk aspiring artists of an identity as creators of works of art and persuade them instead to become dabblers, craftsmen, illustrators, aesthetes, bohemians—anything but to pursue the true and unalloyed identity of artist.

According to certain self-appointed oracles, the artist should be the illustrator of church fable, the servant of religion. To others, the so-called socially conscious group, the artist should serve Marxist realism. Official art of any country is largely government advertising specializing in photo-gloria with no thought of the inherent values of art. Then there are those negative minds which insist that the concept of art was finished with Courbet or Monet or Cubism or Matisse. Finally there are those who make no bones about their hostility to art by telling us that the real art of our time is architecture or the machine.

None of these opinions is anything more than a side-tracking of the real issue, which is the identity of the artist.

The contemporary painter or sculptor sees his identity simply as the producer of the work of art, himself in direct relation to it without any intermediaries. His identity as an artist is concerned with his heritage—his by visual choice and filial position—and the entirely personal nature of what he produces, subject to no outside authority.

The truly creative substance in the work of art is the artist's identity.

How he comes about this is personal. It is internal, secret and slow-growing.

The artist develops his identity by self-confidence. Part can develop by compliment. When that is lacking he can develop the identity defensively. It depends upon his nature and his position, whichever way his conviction is forced to manifest itself. The confidence he may get from critics is usable, but suspect. He is always ready to discard it. He must also develop his identity defensively, even though he may be maturing by compliment, for he knows how easily that can be lost and how tenuous that has been in the past for other artists.

Identity begins with a certain defensive belligerence and at many other times in the artist's life he is forced to use the same means. But the belligerent defense after the inner conviction is acquired is no more a working need but still a weapon in combating adversity.

Sometimes he is aided because he has good teachers and stimulating friends. Sometimes there is no compliment except that which one work gives to another. The defenses necessary to gain identity often become the catalyst to form inner conviction. This is most important, because it is fostering the element of revolt which the artist will use when he reaches full action.

The acknowledged titans are not always most important to him in arriving. While his horizon is narrow, relatively unimportant things or characters fill a niche which the artist's identity needed. It is not axiomatic that the best artists are the best teachers, and his most important influences may come from any source of sincerity. The need within the developing identity will make metaphoric exchange with what is at hand.

The building of identity is recognized among artists and the compliment one artist has for another is more than membership in a mutual assistance society. There is perceptive communication, because artists within the same mores travel the same path in creating, are therefore closer and have a greater appreciation of art than anyone else.

Once identity is made it is stronger than all other authority. The artist is prepared to make his way alone. Aloneness is the condition of the artist's creative life most of the time. The true artist projects into realms that have not been seen and can have only his identity for company. The adventure is alone, and the act of projection is itself actuality. It is himself and the work. He has left behind what was once the subject, as well as other problems of the past, while the people of distinction are still heavily involved in mass form, perspective, beauty, dimension, design, communication, chiaroscuro, social responsibility, and their own limitations of nature.

At maturity, confidence and identity merge. It is not necessarily the

David Smith

opinion of others that cause it. It is the development of the artist in his own mind, by the steps of realization in his works.

This identity must be pure and undivided. Identity can never be two things. It can serve only one master. If the artist is forced to teach or dig ditches for survival, he is the artist who labors temporarily. He does not yield his identity. He does not become the teacher or ditch digger who makes art. He must know that the work of art is the product of one identity created for the great cause of visual response.

Identity determines the artist's finished work before ability. Ability is but one of the attributes and acts only as a degree of identity. Ability might produce a work, but identity makes the works before and the works after. Ability may make the successful work in the eyes of the connoisseurs, but identity makes the failures, which are the most important contribution for the artist. What his critics term the failures are his best works from his own working position. These are closest to actuality and the creative process. These are the works still fluid. It takes time and much verbalizing for the critical viewer to recognize.

He must always be fortified against the rejection of critics. He remembers Delacroix's statements on critics. He remembers the abuse to his own family, the Impressionists, the Fauves and Cubists. He knows that no artist can really be great without having the respect of his fellow artists, but that an artist can be great and have no respect from the museum, the critics or people of authority.

Cézanne, who talked sculpture, finally liberated painting from its perspective illusion. His work around 1900 recognized new purposes which the canvas surface had for painting. Cézanne not only revealed origins which sired Cubism and account for much in the forward art movement today, but equally important was the identity he gave the artist as an independent, free-acting man. He painted with his quick. He responded to insensitive critics by ignoring and withdrawing, not the most judicious behavior for selling, but with the dignity and identity of a sincere artist.

To hold this identity the artist must survey acutely the forces which act for and against him. He must select and reject.

He sees that the great public is beyond his hope. Like Pavlov's dog, they are trained to look only when the bell rings. He needs the public on his terms. They have no need of him.

He knows that no artist lives from museums and that no artist creates art with the conclusions of philosophers and opinions of officials. The museum can compliment the artist's identity if the relationship is one of mutual respect. The artist cannot ask for his recognition, nor will he accept being tolerated.

The artist's only defense is to withdraw from those museums and agencies with whom he is at odds.

The museums and aestheticians will always find among the anxious and unidentified followers who gratefully accept their dogma and tradition, custom and charity. But a growing identity is within the forward movement which will not accept unless the hierarchy responds to the artist's needs instead of determining them.

This position is not new. It is all in the artist's filial heritage, but it is an identity beginning to form and to act.

Notes While Driving

On the way out to Arkansas, 1953,
Highway 60 Illinois

A weathered hawk sitting in a tree
feeling old and slow
feathers gone from the wing
one broken in the tail
watching the 70 mile traffic roar below
thru fields of cotton brush and corn stubble

On the way back,
Arkansas,
1953

It's strange how vulgar curios are and how undefinable is that narrow margin between the total vulgarity of curios and the vulgarity in a creative work of art. The truly creative art is pushing so close to that line of demarcation on which the curio oversteps. An Ozark curio made up of miniature rock specimens from the Ozarks and very vulgar. A Japanese-style donkey meant to be cute. The grouping of a dozen or more curios set in green cement with the open-topped Japanese donkey ostensibly for flowers. The total unity to the artist appears as a very vulgar thing, not even having the basis of function, because its flower use was no more than a tenth of its space taking. Its use for flowers was a minute excuse for display of specimens. Yet all of the specimens were interesting to the artist's eye as objects by themselves, or if presented on a shelf. And if in conscious analyzing the logical reasons of the donkey, the unity only departed in degree.

David Smith

Questions to Students

The following series of questions appears in an undated type-script among the David Smith Papers. Probably written about 1953–54, it accurately reflects Smith's view of the way an artist should approach his work.

1. Do you make art your life, that which always comes first and occupies every moment, the last problem before sleep and the first awaking vision?

2. Do all the things you like or do amplify and enjoin the progress of art vision and art making?

3. Are you a balanced person with many interests and diversions?

4. Do you seek the culture of many aspects, with the middle-class aspiration of being well-rounded and informed?

5. How do you spend your time? More talking about art than making it? How do you spend your money? On art materials first—or do you start to pinch here?

6. How much of the work day or the work week do you devote to your profession—that which will be your identity for life?

7. Will you be an amateur—a professional—or is it the total life?

8. Do you think the artist has an obligation to anyone but himself?

9. Do you think his contemporary position is unique or traditional?

10. Do you think art can be something it was before? Can you challenge the ancients?

11. Have you examined the echoes of childhood and first learning, which may have once given you the solutions? Are any of these expectancies still operating on your choices?

12. Do you hold with these, or have you recognized them? Have you contradicted them or have you made metaphoric transposition?

13. Do you examine and weigh the art statements of fellow artists, teachers, authorities before they become involved in your own working tenets?

14. Or do the useful ideas place themselves in a working niche of your consciousness and the others go off unheard?

15. Do you think you owe your teachers anything, or Picasso or Matisse or Brancusi or Mondrian or Kandinsky?

16. Do you think your work should be aggressive? Do you think this an attribute? Can it be developed?

17. Do you think your work should hold within tradition?

18. Do you think that your own time *and now* is the greatest in the history of art, or do you excuse your own lack of full devotion with the

half belief that some other time would have been better for you to make art?

19. Do you recognize any points of attainment? Do they change? Is there a final goal?

20. In the secret dreams of attainment have you faced each dream for its value on your own basis, or do you harbor inherited aspirations of the bourgeoisie or those of false history or those of critics?

21. Why do you hesitate—why can you not draw objects as freely as you can write their names and speak words about them?

22. What has caused this mental block? If you can name, dream, recall vision and auras why can't you draw them? In the conscious act of drawing, who is acting in your unconscious as censor?

23. In the conceptual direction, are you aiming for the successful work? (To define success I mean the culminating point of many efforts.)

24. Do you aim for a style with a recognizable visual vocabulary?

25. Do you polish up the work beyond its bare aesthetic elements?

26. Do you add ingratiating elements beyond the raw aesthetic basis?

27. If you add ingratiating elements, where is the line which keeps the work from being your own?

28. Are you afraid of rawness, for rawness and harshness are basic forms of U.S. nature, and origins are both raw and vulgar at their time of creation?

29. Will you understand and accept yourself as the subject for creative work, or will your effort go toward adapting your expression to verbal philosophies by non-artists?

30. If you could, would you throw over the present values of harmony and tradition?

31. Do you trust your first response, or do you go back and equivocate consciously? Do you believe that the freshness of first response can be developed and sustained as a working habit?

32. Are you saddled with nature propaganda?

33. Are you afraid to exercise vigor, seek surprise?

34. When you accept the identification of artist do you acknowledge that you are issuing a world challenge in your own time?

35. Are you afraid to work from your own experience without leaning on the crutches of subject and the rational?

36. Or do you think that you are unworthy or that your life has not been dramatic enough or your understanding not classic enough, or do you think that art comes from Mount Parnassus or France or from an elite level beyond you?

37. Do you assert yourself and work in sizes comparable to your physical size or your aesthetic challenge or imagination?

38. Is that size easel-size or table-size or room-size or a challenge to nature?

39. Do you think museums are your friend and do you think they will be interested in your work?

40. Do you think you will ever make a living from museums?

41. Do you think commercial art, architectural art, religious art offer any solution in the maturing of your concepts?

42. How long will you work before you work with the confidence which says, "What I do is art"?

43. Do you ever feel that you don't know where to go in your work, that the challenge is beyond immediate solution?

44. Do you think acclaim can help you? Can you trust it, for you know in your secret self how far short of attainment you always are? Can you trust any acclaim any farther than adverse criticism? Should either have any effect upon you as an artist?

In particular, to the painter—

Is there as much art in a drawing as in a watercolor—or as in an oil painting?

Do you think drawing is a complete and valid approach to art vision, or a preliminary only toward a more noble product?

In particular, to the sculptor—

If a drawing is traced, even with the greatest precision, from another drawing, you will perceive that the one is a copy. Although the differences may deviate less than half a hair, recognizable only by perceptual sensitivity, unanimously we rule the work of the intruder's hand as non-art.

But where is the line of true art—when the sculptor's process often introduces the hands of a plaster caster, the mold maker, the grinder and the polisher, and the patina applier, all these processes and foreign hands intruding deviations upon what was once the original work?

The Artist's Image

This paper was read at a College Art Association meeting in Philadelphia on January 30, 1954.

The greatest force in early twentieth-century American art was against the artist's being the artist. Other forces directed him to be a gentleman, an illustrator, a craftsman, primarily accompanied with apology to

Greece and Italy. The cause of abstract art received a boot both ways from the Armory Show. One hand may count those who held to that heritage which seemed raw, probing, inventive, but which was natural to the way of American life and natural to the way our art should have been made. We have always offended good taste and therein was our heritage. Some tasted the new and deserted to safer beauties, mollification, and adaptation.

The depression and WPA helped the artist toward identity. Through sufferance and picket line, it let him be an artist in certain areas, even an abstract artist. In the thirties, every returning art authority's ashore message announced the death of abstract art. And it appeared dead. The art press rarely mentioned it. It was seldom in museum showing. But a handful held to their heritage. Now, after two wars, abstraction is legion. And occasionally referred to as the bandwagon.

We are born to the heritage of our century, we have chosen a family of pagans from Africa, Oceania, the East, to Altamira. Never in the history of man has the artist's heritage been so great.

Never before has the artist possessed such unique freedom. He pays for this freedom, metal and marble, canvas and color, by means other than sales of his work.

He is pleased that the inheritors of culture refine, polish, and package. How long does it take for crudities to become beauties?

In the making, art is never what *others* say it is or should be. Even when the artist speaks of tangibles they are past and art has gone beyond. He may talk about aims and art without its actually being a determining factor in the work.

If Cézanne's painting had held to his verbal aims it would never have reached such heights.

And now, if the artist works big, it is with cause, and not that the painter is an aspiring muralist, or that the sculptor desires the pedestals of park heroes.

It is his symbol and freedom and identity asserting his stature of the work in ratio to his own being.

It is not packaged and pared to size for concession.

It is the defiant statement of autonomous control.

The artist wonders at judgments, which is masterpiece and which is failure, for each was equal in its making.

That judged failure, still fluid, held most promise for growth. That which was masterpiece, ended and final, fully arrived.

If one is good, why is the other bad? There was nothing qualitative in both their making, both were conceived with the same love.

There is still arrogance and error from all the officials that put him on trial.

David Smith

It is good if he stands guilty of bad art before critics, aestheticians, and historians.

For his work may be free from fastidious indulgences.

And it is very good that the work of art is a lone process.

If art is not what the artist says *he* is, or that which the artist makes, what then is it? It is not the conclusion of the non-artists.

And if you say it is what it was before, there are plenty of artists to meet your demand, willing and anxious cameras.

The image is the aura in space, after the subject is gone—starting a sequence of origins, more pointed than auras.

Or they are visual metaphors of other metaphors transparently overlapped, both humorous and profound.

If it can be seen, why violate vision by saying?

For whom do *you* pass a test—and what is the degree?

There are trains of form reflections, speeding, to form realization more meaningful to the work of art than conscious action.

Reality is the work, there is no subject but the act, reflections in an action of origins.

The creative act is in a constant state of movement; even to try to name its parts would stop its action.

Visual perception without external subject is a part of all action, a constant and daily involvement.

Perception and action are not creatively private or personal, but have become suspect by pragmatists and thus often consciously denied.

Images before they can be named have changed and renewed themselves.

They are still the same in the art-making process as they were thirty millennia back. And the verbalizers are but babes with their words.

Images are part of the values in the work of art, profundities for which there are no identifications.

Identity within man, the artist, the drive and the conviction, make the work of art.

The work of art is not premeditated.

There is movement and cycles of associative influences which are involved right up until the end.

The end may represent only a superficial detachment until it picks up again in the next work.

There was a certain culminating stage reached, but it was not anticipated before the work started.

There is naturally bound to be much error in a verbal interpretation or explanation, especially since all reflection and association are now too far behind to isolate, and which in the first place were visual and never identified.

And in the final analysis all the components are dissolved in the true reality, the work itself.

The Artist and Nature

In the following address, given at the University of Mississippi on March 8, 1955, Smith speaks on the subject of nature and again dwells on the artist's identity.

To talk about nature as the artist's subject has been more the preoccupation of those who do not like to look at art but need easily recognizable objects to talk about. Nature has especially been the harangue of professional critics who lack the courage to oppose openly certain advanced schools of art.

The demand for nature usually boils down to the fact that what is wanted are echoes instead of invention. At times artists talk about nature and state dependence upon it. Some echo the demand made by critical expectancy. Some use the word in their own particular terms with their own meaning. After all, everything that happens in art must happen in nature.

An attitude critical of nature comes from those outside of art making and usually represents a limited vision. Artists learn more from art than from nature. Works of art are more the artist's identity than nature-object identity. But with the change of time, and the change in environment, different artists choose different aspects of nature.

Nature, after all, is everything and everybody. It is impossible for any artist not to be of nature or to deal with problems other than those of nature. On the whole, we are more compassionate than to view nature critically. Being a part of nature we do not question it. We accept it and as one of its elements called creative man, we function.

Reality better represents the artist's term for his position and that, like his own term for nature, includes man the artist along with his imagination. Reality includes the visual memory of all art, and the working reality of his particular art family. The heritage to which he is born is something he knows and accepts as his identity, as one knows and feels his own personal family. His interest in reality is not its prosaic representation but the poetic transposition of it.

Like primitive man, the artist often imagines reality better than he can understand or explain it. In fact, the whole creative process in art flows

David Smith

by vision, without questioning it, without words or even the thought of explanation.

The eidetic image, the after-image, is more important than the object. The associations and their visual patterns are often more important than the object. Ambivalences in visual terms may be more expressive. White is more white when it is dominantly black. Visual metaphoric exchange is perceived daily in many ways. When it is verbalized its poetic value is lost. The mind's eye and not the mirror eye contributes to the perceptual realization of art making more than the reporting view or the idea way.

From the most recent contemporary view the only reality the artist need recognize is that he is the artist. Within this realization he identifies himself as the maker of art, independently, personally, wholly devoted. The maker of art is his nature and his reality. In effect he becomes his own subject matter.

He has not arrived at this position suddenly and alone. It has been a family heritage, especially his art-family of the twentieth century. Impressionism, Post-Impressionism, Fauvism, Cubism, Constructivism, De Stijl, and Surrealism are all in his kinship.

The United States aesthetic at the turn of the century was dependent upon the European. Most of our artists studied in Paris, the art center of Europe, encountered, followed, or contributed to the various new and revolutionary ways art was forming. Beginning in 1909, Stieglitz's gallery in New York exhibited some returning painters essentially influenced by Post-Impressionism, namely Weber, Hartley, Maurer, [Bernard] Karfiol, and [Samuel] Halpert. This was the beginning of our change. After the Armory Show in 1913 early Cubism introduced another vision to accompany Post-Impressionism. For a short time these two movements stimulated United States artists to a semi-abstract position. The sculptors Archipenko, Laurent, and Lachaise became United States residents, bodily moving their work and views into the academy conservatism of the United States sculpture scene. There was no unifying stimulus and little public support. The conviction of the new view for most of the artists was not deep enough to last long. The concept of Cubism was still fluid, and not well defined—some of our painters got waylaid with Italian Futurism, its speed and machines which, in a way, was more definite due to the manifestos, writings, and organized effort. Most of our painters worked with a realist concept, applying a Futurist or Cubist rendering. Until 1940, the abstract painters or sculptors in our country could be counted in single numbers.

After 1946, the abstract painters and sculptors blossomed by thousands. With 1950, a new movement, yet unnamed for certain, but most often referred to as "Abstract Expressionism," developed without manifesto or organization, indigenous and independent, the United States's first native art movement. The history of this is in process, the situation is still fluid. Claims are made that France had a simultaneous movement, but I believe history will show our lead. Some of the French critics have given this credit to us.

This movement in the United States was much like Cubism in France. Cubism was not an organized movement, but those who participated in it agree that its collective result came from each man's individual poetic vision and wholly within his own nature. Cubism did not include all the great artists and innovators in Europe at its peak of 1910–14 any more than Abstract Expressionism includes all the truly creative work in the United States up to 1955. The reference to schools by either name is most general.

It doesn't matter particularly whether the French or United States artists were first. We have come of age, and intuitively create with an autonomous conviction. I couldn't begin to name these new-order painters and sculptors. There are thousands. Their number increases steadily in all parts of the country.

The masters, Picasso, Matisse, Bonnard, Rouault, Brancusi, Braque, etc., have stayed the masters. We are their inheritors as much as their own countrymen or the countries in which they have chosen to live.

Many Europeans have come to our country either as guests or refugees—Chagall, Léger, Miró, Masson, Klee, Moore, Brancusi, and many others. Even as visitors, they have fortified our art. Others like Lipchitz, Mondrian, Gabo, Duchamp have become United States residents, bringing part of the international heritage to our country. Nothing in particular, but in general many things have made our environment.

I suppose historians will be able to find reasons to suit their needs why we have happened, but I hope we are eclipsed as the relative beginning of a greater movement.

As we stand, we have no dependence upon the outsiders who say what art is, was, or should be. We realize that the aestheticians only can speak after the act of art. We are always ahead, and further separated from them by the fact that the heritage of our art is always visual and not verbal. The theory-laden historians truth-beauty calculations of past ages have no connection with us.

We work with our own convictions. We will stand or fall with the confidence that art is what we make.

Painting carried the creative banner at the turn of the century. Brancusi, our greatest living sculptor, was the only exception. Cubism, essentially a sculptural concept originated by painters, did more for sculpture than any other influence. Besides, some of the greatest departures in sculpture were made by painters. Both Picasso and Matisse contributed works with origins quite outside the sculptor's concept. Picasso made the first Cubist head in 1909. It was Picasso, working with another Spaniard, González, in 1929, who made the iron constructions utilizing "found" or collected objects.

Cubism freed sculpture from monolithic and volumetric form as Impressionism freed painting from chiaroscuro. The poetic vision in sculpture is fully as free as in painting. Like a painting, sculpture now deals in the illusion of form as well as its own particular property of form itself. Both new vision and new material have contributed importances and new paths. But certainly what is most important on our scene is the identity the artist has attained.

Drawing

This lecture on drawing was developed from class notes and delivered at a forum conducted by George Rickey at Sophie Newcomb College, Tulane University, on March 21, 1955.

Many students think of drawing as something hasty and preparatory before painting or making sculpture. A sort of purgatory between amateurism and accomplishment. As a preliminary before the great act, because everybody can draw some, and children are uninhibited about it and do it so easily, and writing itself is a style of drawing, and it is common on sidewalks, board fences, phone booths, etc.

But actually only a very experienced artist may appreciate the challenge, because it is so common an expression. It is also the most revealing, having no high expectancy to maintain, not even the authenticating quality of gold frames to artificially price or lend grandeur to its atmosphere. And, by its very conditioning, it comes much closer to the actual bareness of the soul and the nature of free expressionism.

It is not expected to carry the flourish, the professionalism of oil painting, nor the accuracy and mannered clarity in the formal brushing of the watercolorist.

If it is pompous, artificial, pretentious, insincere, mannered, it is so evident, so quick to be detected, and like the written line, it is a quickly recognized key to personality. If it is timid, weak, overbold or blustering, it is revealed much as one perceives it in the letter or a signature. There is not the demand or tradition for technique and conformity. The pureness of statement, the honesty of expression, is laid bare in a black-and-white answer of who that mark-maker is, what he stands for, how strong his conviction, or how weak. Often his true personality is revealed before repetitions or safer symbols can come to his defense. More his truth than other media with technique and tradition, more his truth than words can express, more free from thinking in words than polished techniques, drawing is more shaped like he is shaped, because the pressure of performance has not made him something he isn't.

The drawing that comes from the serious hand can be unwieldy, uneducated, unstyled and still be great simply by the superextension of whatever conviction the artist's hand projects and being so strong that it eclipses the standard qualities critically expected. The need, the drive to express can be so strong that the drawing makes its own reason for being.

Drawing is the most direct, closest to the true self, the most natural liberation of man—and if I may guess back to the action of very early man, it may have been the first celebration of man with his secret self— even before song.

But its need doesn't stand on primitive reconstruction—anyone knows, everyone feels the need to draw. I truly believe that anything anyone has seen he can draw, and that everyone here has now seen everything he ever will see, and that all that stands between his drawing anything in the world is his own inhibition. What that is we don't know. Each must dig himself out of his own mind and liberate the act of drawing to the vision of memory. It is not so much that this correlation is impossible—but more the mental block that keeps him from trying that which he deems impossible.

We are blocked from creative ways of expressing by ways we feel about things and by ways we think we ought to feel, by word pictures that cancel out creative vision, and intimidations that limit creative expression.

If drawing could come now as easily as when a man was six, he would not doubt or think, he would do. But since he approaches it more consciously and not with the child's freedom, he must admit to himself that he is making a drawing—and he approaches mark-making humbly, self-consciously, or timidly. Here he finds pressure and intimidation and inhibition. But the first mark of drawing is made. Sometimes it takes courage to make this one statement. This stroke is as good as he can make, now. The next and those to come lead toward creative freedom. He must try to be himself in the stroke. He dominates the line related to image and does not permit the image to dominate him and the line. Not a line the way others think the line should be—not how history says it once was; nor what multitudes say they cannot do with a straight line. For a line so drawn with conviction is straighter in context than the ruler.

David Smith

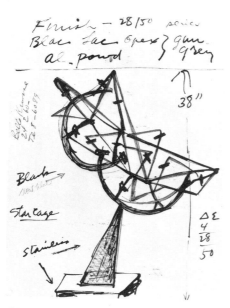

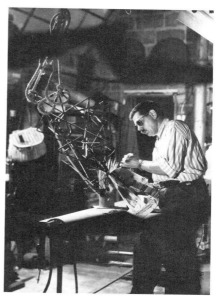

34. Preliminary sketch for *Star Cage,* in
    a notebook of c. 1944–54.

35. David Smith at work on *Star Cage,*
    1950.

36. *Star Cage,* 1950. Steel painted midnight blue, 45 x 52½ x 28 inches.
    John Rood Sculpture Collection, University Gallery, University of
    Minnesota, Minneapolis. Photograph by David Smith.

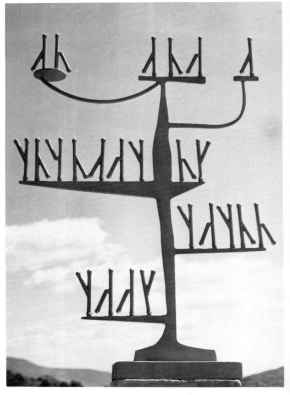

38. *The Forest,* 1950. Steel painted green, pink, 37 x 29 x 4 inches. Private collection. Photograph by David Smith.

37. *24 Greek Y's,* 1950. Steel painted green, 42¾ x 29⅛ x 4 inches. The Museum of Modern Art, New York; Blanchette Rockefeller Fund. Photograph by David Smith.

39. *The Fish,* in progress at the Bolton Landing shop, 1950. Photograph by David Smith.

40. *The Fish,* 1950. Steel painted scarlet, 68 x 69⅝ x 18 inches. Private collection. Photograph by David Smith.

41. *The Letter,* 1950. Welded steel, 37⅝ x 22⅞ x 9¼ inches. Munson-Williams-Proctor Institute, Utica, New York. Photograph by David Smith.

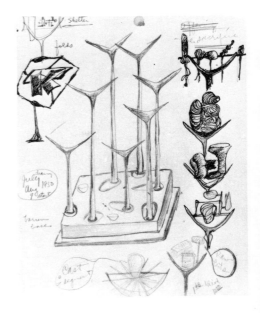

(right)

42. Preliminary sketches for *Sacrifice,* in a notebook of c. 1950–54.

(opposite)

43. *Sacrifice,* 1950. Steel painted red, 31⅝ x 19⅝ x 20⅞ inches. Collection Mr. and Mrs. Harold E. Rayburn. Photograph by David Smith.

44. *Song of a Landscape,* 1950. Steel, 24½ x 33¾ x 19¼ inches. Collection Muriel K. Newman. Photograph by David Smith.

45. *Cathedral,* 1950. Steel painted brown, 34⅜ x 24½ x 17⅛ inches. Collection McCrory Corporation, New York. Photograph by David Smith.

46. *Australia,* 1951. Steel painted brown, 79¾ x 107 x 16¾ inches. The Museum of Modern Art, New York; Fractional gift from William S. Rubin.

47. *Hudson River Landscape,* 1951. Steel, stainless steel, 49½ x 75 x 16½ inches. Whitney Museum of American Art, New York. Photograph by David Smith.

48. *Agricola V,* 1952. Steel, 35½ inches high x 28 inches wide. Collection Mr. and Mrs. Eugene M. Schwartz. Photograph by David Smith.

49. *Agricola VIII,* 1952. Steel, bronze painted brown, 31¾ x 21¼ x 18¾ inches. Estate of the artist. Photograph by David Smith.

50. *Tanktotem IV,* 1953 (left). Steel, 92½ x 33⅜ x 29 inches. Albright-Knox Art Gallery, Buffalo, New York. *Tanktotem III,* 1953 (right). Steel, 84½ x 27 x 20 inches. Estate of the artist. Photograph by David Smith.

51. *Parallel 42,* 1953. Steel, 53½ x 26 x 19 inches. Estate of the artist. Photograph by David Smith.

52. *Cubi IX,* 1961. Stainless steel, 106¼ x 56 x 46 inches. Walker Art Center, Minneapolis. Photograph by David Smith.

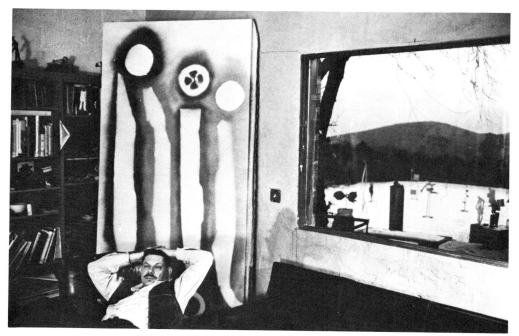

53. David Smith at Bolton Landing. Photograph by Dan Budnick, 1962.

54. David Smith at work on the Voltri-Bolton
series, Bolton Landing. *Voltri-Bolton VIII* on
floor, right. Photograph by Dan Budnick,
1962.

56. *Voltri XXI,* 1962 (left). Steel, 51 x 26¼ x 25 inches. The Hirshhorn Museum and Sculpture Garden, Smithsonian Institution. *Voltri XX,* 1962 (right). Steel, 77¾ x 27¼ x 9⅜ inches. Collection Mr. and Mrs. Robert Schwartz. Photograph by David Smith, Spoleto, Italy, 1962.

(opposite)
55. *Voltri XVIII,* 1962 (left rear). Steel, 95 x 31⅜ x 29¾ inches. Estate of the artist. *Voltri IV,* 1962 (center rear). Steel, 68½ x 59¾ x 14½ inches. Kröler-Müller Stichting, Otterlo, Netherlands. *Voltri V,* 1962 (right front). Steel, 86⅝ x 39½ x 21¾ inches. The Hirshhorn Museum and Sculpture Garden, Smithsonian Institution. Photograph by David Smith, Spoleto, Italy, 1962.

(right)
57. Factory at Voltri, Italy. Photograph by David Smith, 1962.

58. *Primo Piano I,* 1962. Steel painted white, 110 x 144 x 21 inches. Collection David Mirvish Gallery, Toronto. Photograph by David Smith.

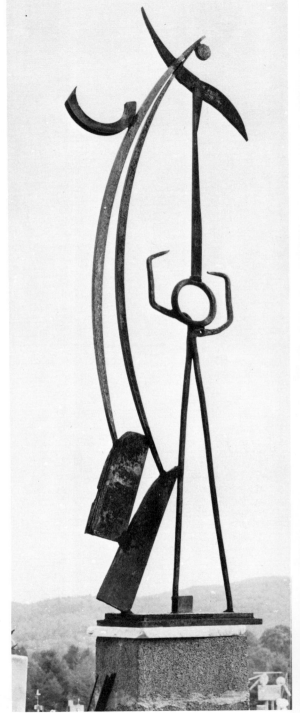

59. *Voltri-Bolton VIII,* 1962. Steel, 90 x 6 x 1½ inches. Collection Mr. and Mrs. Robertson F. Alford. Photograph by David Smith.

60. Sculpture in a field at Bolton Landing. Photograph by Garnett McCoy, 1965.

61. *Cubi XXIII,* 1964. Stainless steel, 76¼ x 172⅞ x 26¾ inches. Los Angeles County Museum of Art; Contemporary Art Council Fund. Photograph by David Smith.

62. *Cubi XVIII,* 1964 (left). Stainless steel, 107 x 21¾ x 20 inches. Museum of Fine Arts, Boston. *Cubi XVII,* 1963 (center). Stainless steel, 107¾ x 64⅞ x 38⅛ inches. Dallas Museum of Fine Arts; The Eugene and Margaret McDermott Fund. *Cubi XIX,* 1964 (right). Stainless steel, 113⅛ x 21¾ x 20¾ inches. The Tate Gallery, London. Photograph by David Smith.

The deviations outside mechanical realism, which, usually with a bit of hostility, represent the average expectancy, are the nature of human line—the inaccuracies, so-called, are often other images trying to assert themselves in association. And the truth of image is not single, it is many—the image in memory is many actions and many things—often trying to express its subtle overlapping in only one line or shape.

Simply stated, the line is a personal-choice line. The first stroke demands another in complement, the second may demand the third in opposition, and the approach continues, each stroke more free because confidence is built by effort. If the interest in this line gesture making is sustained, and the freedom of the act developed, realization to almost any answer can be attained. Soon confidence is developed and one of the secrets of drawing felt, and marks come so easily and move so fast that no time is left to think.

Even the drawing made before the performance is often greater, more truthful, more sincere than the formal production later made from it. Such a statement will find more agreement with artists than from connoisseurs. Drawings usually are not pompous enough to be called works of art. They are often too truthful. Their appreciation neglected, drawings remain the life force of the artist.

Especially is this true for the sculptor, who, of necessity, works in media slow to take realization. And where the original creative impetus must be maintained during labor, drawing is the fast-moving search which keeps physical labor in balance.

González: First Master of the Torch

The pioneering welded sculpture that Julio González began executing in the 1920's was perhaps the single most important influence on the development of David Smith's work. Smith frequently acknowledged his debt to González, and in this article, published in Art News *in February, 1956, pays tribute to the Spanish artist.*

The Bull in its symbolic action has stood for many things in Picasso's history, things Spanish and things noble. The Bull has been the artist, the people of Spain, the open-eyed conscience of free men, the disemboweler of the lie of Franco, the aggressive protector of women, and among other symbols, the lover of woman.

But after the death of Julio González, Picasso's friend of forty-five years, the Bull becomes a skull on a green and blue fractioned table before the window curtained in violet and black.

Coming home from the funeral Picasso had done this picture of a bull's skull and dedicated it: *"En hommage à González."*

To the wall of his studio was tacked a snapshot of his friend. For Picasso all source of life becomes the nature of painting.

On what peaks did memory ride—for they were friends from youth, from the days of the Barcelona café, Els Quatre Gats. In 1901 Picasso shared González's living-quarters in Paris until he found a studio. Throughout the succeeding years they remained on good terms, visiting each other, even working together; and then, the end at Arcueil in March of 1942.

The youngest of four children (the others, his sisters Pilar and Lola, his brother Juan), González was born in Barcelona in 1876. Both Juan and Julio were apprenticed in their father's metal shop, becoming third-generation smiths. With other ideas in mind, the brothers studied painting at night at the Barcelona School of Fine Arts, which Miró was to attend fifteen years later. They knew Els Quatre Gats, the Spanish counterpart of the Parisian Chat Noir and gathering point of the local avant-garde. Here the youthful Picasso had decorated the walls with twenty-five portraits of writers and artists who frequented the café.

During the 1890's the tension between the impoverished multitudes and the wealthy few of prosperous Barcelona manifested itself in a series of strikes, reprisals, and acts of anarchy. Dispossessed refugees pouring in from Cuba increased the degree and extent of the economic problem.

The intellectual reaction to the social distress and rebellious temper of the times was to revolt against tradition and authority and embrace the attitudes of "modernism." Thus Barcelona awoke to the romanticism of the age, Art Nouveau, the Gothic Revival, Wagner's music, Lautrec's presentation of Paris and the bohemian life, Maeterlinck's drama, the Pre-Raphaelites, and the climaxing monument to the new art, Gaudí's cathedral.

I feel González coming from Barcelona and looking back lovingly at Gaudí's cathedral of the Sagrada Familia, respecting Gaudí's source in nature and the unities of iron and stone.

González's notebook contains statements about the new art which seem almost parallel ideals for the Catalonian Gaudí's cathedral: "To project and draw in space with new methods . . . Only the pinnacle of a cathedral can show us where the soul can rest suspended . . . These points in infinity were the precursors of the new art." In another reference to a cathedral he speaks of "the motionless arrow" which to me seems more the arrowhead Excelsis Hosanna towers of Sagrada Familia

David Smith

than the Gothic or Romanesque spires which he loved in France. His notes several times speak of form by established "points or perforations." There is a marked unity in his stone bases and the iron sculpture, a sensitive feeling for material and proportion. I feel the kinship with Gaudí's stone angels, their iron trumpets and iron arm supports, in the feeling of flying form and unorthodox balance. Work by the González shop may even be in the cathedral. I can find no verification for this, but José de Creeft, who worked on it as a plasterer's helper at the age of twelve, says that every craftsman in Barcelona did.

The craft work of both brothers progressed so well that it was shown in the Chicago World's Fair, 1893, and in the same year took a gold medal in the Barcelona Exposition.

The period from his arrival in Paris around 1899 until 1927 did not show strong sculptural conviction. This, perhaps the most difficult and dramatic period of his life, was the least fruitful. Unproductive months followed the death of his brother. Then, repoussé masks, drawings, and paintings proceeded out of his struggle for some fifteen years.

There seems to have been conflict between the divided identities of painter and metalsmith.

When a man is trained in metal-working and has pursued it as labor with the ideal of art represented by oil painting, it is very difficult to conceive that what has been labor and livelihood is the same means by which art can be made. (Perhaps I am basing this more on sympathy than fact in González's case, because it is a reconstruction of my own experience. Before I had painted very long I ran across reproductions in *Cahiers d'Art* of González's and Picasso's work which brought my consciousness to this fact that art could be made of iron. But iron-working was labor, when I thought art was oil paint.)

In this period of groping, González felt the need of men strong and firm in their destiny, like Brancusi and Picasso. Undoubtedly their encouragement played a part in his slow battle with himself. At the same time the very closeness to these two titans personally could not permit any influence in his own work.

It seems true that something kept his painting from flowering. At the same time he pursued metal work, which apparently represented the sculptural part of his nature before it had asserted its singular self. From the chronology of his life and from the knowledge of friends, as soon as he accepted his true identity as that of the sculptor, his expression became more challenging and his works more prolific. Concurrent to this came the use of the acetylene torch, which was not, I think, a part of his early apprenticeship or of the metal-craft period.

He was past fifty when he accepted the sculptor's identity, discarded the silversmith's scale and purpose, and abandoned oil painting formally, accepting drawing as the complement of sculpture. Some of the finer parts of craftsmanship were dropped, a casual approach technically developed with the dominance of conceptual ends. Craft and smithery became submerged in the concept of sculpture. The aesthetic end was not dependent upon its mode of travel.

The period in which González worked for Picasso has not been determined by the statement of either as far as I can learn. It does not seem important. The technical collaboration made neither change nor influence in the conception of either artist. During the several years it existed, each pursued his own work in his own way, Picasso with his concepts for Mediterranean monument houses, the elongated bronze stick figures, etc.; González reaching his prolific period with *Don Quixote,* a number of still lifes, the best of his masks, and a large number of flying iron drawings, like *Standing Personage* and *Woman Combing Her Hair.* The possible dates of this intermittent collaboration lie somewhere between 1928 and 1932.

González was encouraged by Picasso to continue and expand; something very definite was gained by their union, but it was more abstract than a recognizable influence.

The best of González is in his abstract work, but existing concomitantly is a socially conscious theme of realism. These are the *Montserrats* or her variations. They start in 1932 with a small head, *Montserrat,* continue to the full-sized figure in 1936 and end with a bronze head in 1942. *La Montserrat* is the symbol of Catalonian woman in her nobility, her cries against injustice, her suffering. She is the symbol of things noble and things Spanish, analogous to Picasso's bull.

Of the two unfinished plaster works begun in 1941, one was abstract; the other a screaming woman on her knees, which parallels the *Montserrat* series in its realism and sympathy.

I have learned of no notes relating to the realist approach. There are no poetic "directions to carve space," no "motionless arrows pointing toward the stars where the soul can rest suspended or indicate points of hope," as he gives his ideals for sculpture. These are volume sculptures, arrived at with great love and patience. They show the tremendous urge to speak out in the way the quiet man and artist could best present his statement.

A man as withdrawn as González was ordinarily not given to fraternizing. An exception was his attendance at weekly meetings held at the studio of Torres García in the late twenties and early thirties. To these discussion evenings came an interesting group, mostly young, almost exclusively expatriate: Mondrian, Arp, Bissière (later Hélion), van Doesburg, Seuphor, Daura, Xceron, John Graham, Vantongerloo, Queto, Charchoune, Cyaky, Brummer, and others. From the same address was published the magazine *Cercle et Carré,* edited by García and Seuphor. The painter Xceron, then writing art reviews for the Paris edition of the *Chicago Tribune,* was probably the first American to write about González's work, which he did most favorably and understandingly. Graham, another painter-member of the group, was probably the first American to buy González's sculpture. The three pieces he bought in 1930 were, as far as I know, the first in this country.

A. E. Gallatin, who was known to most of this group, in 1934 bought a silver sculpture done two years earlier and a drawing for his Museum of Living Art. Graham describes the noted sculptor as he remembers him in 1930: "Small, dignified, dressed in black like a real Mediterranean, lean, graying, a quiet and modest person, dreamy and detached, in the way of many thoughtful Spanish men, an attractive person looking more in than out. He commanded sympathy and respect."

One of those who knew him best during the last years of his life was Henri Goetz, an American painter living in France. In 1937 Goetz became acquainted with González, his wife and sisters through Hans Hartung, who married the sculptor's daughter Roberta. A strong family friendship developed, with Sunday dinners at Arcueil in the house González had built according to his own plans, and drives through the countryside to look at Gothic churches in an old Citroën González bought in 1938. Indicating the sculptor's gentle humor, Goetz recalls the way he used to pass the weekly dish of carrots and slyly say, "Do take a wing."

González was not much given to art talk or theory and in these family discussions of abstraction, Mondrian, Kandinsky, etc., he was at aesthetic odds with Hartung and Goetz, who took the favorable view.

In one of his infrequent confidences of an aesthetic nature he told Goetz that he sometimes used the Golden Section (1.6180). This mathematical ideal of the relationship of the diagonal with the side of the square may be homage to Cézanne and the 1912 *Section d'or* exhibition, or something very personal from his painting period. The Golden Section has always been a constant in the eye of man. It may have been a personal method of evaluating, but it is certainly not the inspiration.

Regarding his own work González was adamant in pointing out the relationship between his sculpture and the real elements—such as hair, teeth, eyes—which in a very indirect way composed them. Goetz recalls his buying what was for his circumstances a very costly tool—possibly a shearing tool—to work on the teeth of a sculpture. The beautiful head of 1936 which Alfred Barr acquired in 1937 from Christian Zervos for the Museum of Modern Art collection clearly illustrates his preoccupation with features.

González was extremely prudent. Early in the war he gave up welding, fearing that if bombs dropped his oxygen and acetylene tanks would blow up, although the lorry factory less than a hundred yards away had many tanks in constant use.

González never became a French citizen. He was Spanish, but insisted on the distinction of being a Catalonian.

Critical accent has been placed upon who was first in iron or welding. This speculation is no more valid than the Renaissance oil paint controversy. González was an apprentice in his father's shop, his work with metal starts in childhood. It is not innovation that makes art but inspiration. On the relationship with Picasso, Xceron recalls that he came to González's studio in Rue de Médée around 1928 to work on the statue for the tomb of Apollinaire. In Picasso's iron sculpture the concept and the forms are strictly his, as are González's in his own work. With Gargallo, whom González instructed, the technique becomes developed in a spectacular way, but the concept remains essentially academic.

The Cubists used iron (i.e., Laurens's *Composition,* 1914) as did the Constructivists (Tatlin in 1917, Meduniezky in 1919, etc.). De Creeft made an iron stovepipe *Don Quixote* in 1925; Lipchitz told me of a 1928 iron sculpture he exhibited in his 1930 Paris retrospective show. No one was first. All materials have properties by which they are shaped; art lies in the concept, not the technique. You can find more art in paper scraps than in crafted gold.

Wrought metal sculpture goes back to the Bulls of Al 'Ubaid (3000 B.C.) and the life-sized figure of Pepi I from Hierakonpolis (2300 B.C.). A whole age of iron welding and forming flowered in Syria in the eleventh to ninth century B.C. The iron headrest of Tutankhamen (1350 B.C.), believed to have come from Syria, was welded. In Genesis, Tubal Cain, husband of Zilah, is referred to as the instructor of every artificer in bronze and iron. Iron welding and working has been in evidence in almost every period of culture in both art and function.

The Artist and the Architect

These thoughts on the relationship between architects on the one hand and painters and sculptors on the other were given as the Alcoa Foundation Lecture at Rensselaer Polytechnic Institute, Troy, New York, on November 20, 1957.

Not too many years ago in Germany the hope was expressed that architecture and art might collaborate and enrich each other. The inaugural

David Smith

manifesto of the Bauhaus declared: "We must desire, imagine, and work together for the institution of the future in which architecture, sculpture, and painting will combine in harmony."

To desire, imagine, and work together in harmony is a marvel in idealism which may have succeeded to some degree within their own school. But it is hard to say that Klee, Feininger, or Albers influenced later architecture, or that Gropius and Breuer affected the course of experiment in art. The contribution of these men from the Bauhaus seems to be found in the identity of each, as artist or architect.

The art historian has developed a myth (because both employ form) that brotherhood and joint need should bring together artist and architect in a working relationship. This academic fancy of kinship and dependence is still heard and read, despite the obvious difference in viewpoint, ethics, means of production, and nature of the professions.

There is no cultural or moral mandate saying architects should support artists. Even so, had the affinity the art historians talk of existed, the architect's practice would be to use art as art in buildings, instead of art as decorative detail or afterthought. No truly notable place has been found for Lipchitz, a sculptor in the monumental vein. Mondrian was similarly neglected, although ironically his ideas were taken over and worked for architectural purposes. If these men with already secure positions in art history have been overlooked, how can painters and sculptors who have not reached their eminence consider architecture in their future?

This lack of interest in each other's ideas is not recent. Since the days of Impressionism, art and architecture have proceeded independently. Great and original art was being made in the late nineteenth and early twentieth centuries, while planners of buildings were occupied with imitation Gothic, Romanesque, Renaissance—designing their own sculptural banalities and commissioning artless anecdotes. Monet, Rodin, Seurat, Gauguin, Picasso, Matisse, and Brancusi, with their mastery of the vast size, were naturally suited to the space of architecture.

Of course, architects do approach painters and sculptors. A sculptor recognized in the art world will on occasion be asked to submit sketches on speculation, without fee. Usually the architects don't know enough about art or artists and have to ask museums for a list. There are competitions for commissions, a gamble few can afford. Consequently, these do not attract the best, and the winning entries are considered poor within the art profession.

Once an architect, professing interest in an early sculpture, asked to retain the photograph. The only result of this was that some time later a glass-topped table appeared with a base very like my sculpture turned sideways. This was a detail for a newly designed house in Long Island.

Years ago this even then successful architect leafed through a book of a European fair, showed me an illustration, and wondered if I couldn't do something like it about fifteen feet high for $1,500. My point is not the money, but the ethics of lifting, which to him was just competitive business.

When the world's noblest building was proposed, there was no echo of the Bauhaus dictum. A collective of the world's most noted architects planned it exclusive of painters and sculptors. When completed, it had some folk art, a blown-up copy of a Léger painting, and an architect-designed background for the podium which some of the younger architects referred to as a wall of police buttons. As I learned subsequently, five of us were given individual tours for suggestions or commissions to do remedial work on the police-button effect. The architect failed to foresee that none of us would be interested in a job that was not sculpture but redesigning.

In current practice the designer seems to fill the architect's need better than the painter or sculptor. Designers are paid less, work faster, are more amenable in adhering to the decor. Designers can make the compromise with something that looks like art but stays with the building. As long as the architect can direct elements, even the designer will not usurp his space or challenge his purity. He has nothing like this certainty with a sculptor, whose whole outlook and history have not accustomed him to the demands of commercial designing. If his work does not contain his full identity and represent his own aesthetic convictions, it may show up as a weak compromise.

Architects often imply that art prices are too high. Generally speaking they are considerably below the architect's scale. The big architect betrays a touch of condescension in his attitude, as if aware of himself as the Gothic master builder dealing with just another one of the craftsmen. My impression has been that no strong desire for the work existed, and that I was expected to price the work low out of gratefulness for the chance to have people see it. Avant-garde sculptors and painters commissioned for abstract work in some of the new religious buildings have found that when their figures were all in, they had made equal to or less than plumbers' wages. These were small buildings, supported by small congregations. Had it been a big job with a big firm, probably the architects would have designed out the need for creative artists.

If it is true that the architect rarely calls for his services, it is also true that the artist does not make work with architecture as a frame of reference. But it is more than this. It is an encompassing difference in aims, methods, and ends.

For most artists in the last hundred years, the struggle has been hard, but with it has come a conceptual freedom and independence enjoyed

David Smith

by few other professions, and a gradual ripening and developing of a true art identity. This identity permits the artist today to work from his inner responses, not even beholden to nature, except as he the artist reflects it. For an artist in this country, the absence of a cultural history is not the blight it once was, nor is the achievement of past European art any longer an intimidation. For the first time in our short history, the art is so strong that its influence is felt abroad. At this moment the art of this country does without the polish, seductiveness, and packaging of the Europeans, having an aggressive vigor and a rawness approaching vulgarity. If the statement is powerful and demanding, the vulgarities will be recognized as beauties.

Our nature and ideology run counter to the architect's obligations. He must deal in immediate beauties. To execute his work he must sell it beforehand, while the artist may take a lifetime or longer to have his vulgarities revealed as beauties.

Big architecture becomes increasingly complex and collective. The sculptor's method of operation is just the opposite. Even the practice of editions of sculpture has almost disappeared. Instead of producing duplicate bronzes from the original plaster, sculptors are producing one direct original in metal. This permits more direct action in working, a sustained continuity to completion, and the entire elimination of any marks of labor on the work except his own. Like the painter's, his work is unique, a copy would seem unethical. In addition, reproductions or copies take time. Having accepted the challenge of ideas, he is not content with a past position of performance on a static concept. Like the painter, he is interested in the speed of ideas and upon each work drives to project his concept still further.

There are architects who believe that architecture is the bona fide sculpture of today. The sculptor can only differ in opinion, replying that sculpture is made for visual aesthetic response, essentially executed by one man, that it serves no physical function and doesn't have to be conceived with allowance for indoor plumbing.

Sometimes architects defend the myth that architecture is the mother of all fine art. Wright less than two weeks ago publicly implied that painting and sculpture are dependents of architecture. Corbusier has painted his murals and designed his sculpture. We know the attempts of Wallace Harrison at painting and sculpture.

There is no ideal union of art and architecture when art is needed simply to fill a hole or enliven a dead wall. Good architecture does not need art if the architect himself doesn't see it in his conception, feel it as a complement. Good sculpture has its own form. It is based upon a different aesthetic structure. Until the architect gives up the preconception that sculpture is merely another of his details and accepts it on its own terms, seeks it as one contemporary autonomy meeting another in a relationship of aesthetic strength and excellence, art and architecture will remain the strangers they have been for at least the last hundred years.

Tradition and Identity

The following speech was given on April 17, 1959, at Ohio University in Athens, Ohio, which Smith attended for a year in 1924–25.

When I lived and studied in Ohio, I had a very vague sense of what art was. Everyone I knew who used the reverent word was almost as unsure and insecure.

Mostly art was reproductions, from far away, from an age past and from some golden shore, certainly from no place like the mud banks of the Auglaze or the Maumee, and there didn't seem much chance that it could come from Paulding County.

Genuine oil painting was some highly cultivated act that came like the silver spoon, born from years of slow method, applied drawing, watercoloring, designing, art structure, requiring special equipment of an almost secret nature, that could only be found in Paris or possibly New York, and when I got to New York and Paris I found that painting was made with anything at hand, building board, raw canvas, self-primed canvas, with or without brushes, on the easel, on the floor, on the wall, no rules, no secret equipment, no anything, except the conviction of the artist, his challenge to the world and his own identity.

Discarding the old methods and equipment will not of course make art. It has only been a symbol in creative freedom from the bondage of tradition and outside authority.

Sculpture was even farther away. Modeling clay was a mystic mess which came from afar. How sculpture got into metal was so complex that it could be done only in Paris. The person who made sculpture was someone else, an ethereal poetic character divinely sent, who was scholar, aesthetician, philosopher, Continental gentleman so sensitive he could unlock the crying vision from a log or a Galatea from a piece of imported marble.

I now know that sculpture is made from rough externals by rough characters or men who have passed through all polish and are back to the rough again.

The mystic modeling clay is only Ohio mud, the tools are at hand in garages and factories. Casting can be achieved in almost every town. Visions are from the imaginative mind, sculpture can come from the found discards in nature, from sticks and stones and parts and pieces, assembled or monolithic, solid form, open form, lines of form, or, like a painting, the illusion of form. And sculpture can be painting and painting can be sculpture and no authority can overrule the artist in his declaration. Not even the philosopher, the aesthetician, or the connoisseur.

I have spoken against tradition, but only the tradition of others who would hold art from moving forward. Tradition holding us to the perfections of others. In this context tradition can only say what art was, not what art is. Tradition comes wrapped in word pictures; these are traps which lead laymen into cliché thinking. This leads to analogy and comparative evaluation and conclusion, especially in the hands of historians. Where conclusions are felt, the understanding of art has been hampered and the innovations of the contemporary scene are often damned.

Art has its tradition, but it is a visual heritage. The artist's language is the memory from sight. Art is made from dreams, and visions, and things not known, and least of all from things that can be said. It comes from the inside of who you are when you face yourself. It is an inner declaration of purpose, it is a factor which determines artist identity.

The nature to which we all refer in the history of art is still with us, although somewhat changed; it is no longer anecdote or robed and blindfolded virtue, the bowl of fruit, or that very abstract reference called realistic; it is very often the simple subject called the artist. Identifying himself as the artist, he becomes his own subject as one of the elements in nature. He no longer dissects it, nor moralizes upon it; he is its part. The outside world of nature is equal, without accent, unquestioning. He is an element in the atmosphere called nature, his reference to nature is more like primitive man addressing it as "thou" and not "it." Aura and association, all the parts into the whole expression, all actions in an emotional flow, manifest the artist as subject, a new position for the artist but natural to his time. Words become difficult, they can do little in explaining a work of art, let alone the position of the artist in the creative irrational flow of power and force which underlies the position and conception. Possibly I can explain my own procedure more easily. When I begin a sculpture I'm not always sure how it is going to end. In a way it has a relationship to the work before, it is in continuity with the previous work—it often holds a promise or a gesture toward the one to follow.

I do not often follow its path from a previously conceived drawing. If I have a strong feeling about its start, I do not need to know its end; the battle for solution is the most important. If the end of the work seems too complete and final, posing no question, I am apt to work back from the end, that in its finality it poses a question and not a solution.

Sometimes when I start a sculpture I begin with only a realized part; the rest is travel to be unfolded, much in the order of a dream.

The conflict for realization is what makes art, not its certainty, its technique, or material. I do not look for total success. If a part is successful, the rest clumsy or incomplete, I can still call it finished, if I've said anything new, by finding any relationship which I might call an origin.

I will not change an error if it feels right, for the error is more human than perfection. I do not seek answers. I haven't named this work nor thought where it would go. I haven't thought what it is for, except that it is made to be seen. I've made it because it comes closer to saying who I am than any other method I can use. This work is my identity. There were no words in my mind during its creation, and I'm certain words are not needed in its seeing; and why should you expect understanding when I do not? That is the marvel—to question but not to understand. Seeing is the true language of perception. Understanding is for words. As far as I am concerned, after I've made the work, I've said everything I can say.

Memories to Myself

The following speech was given at the Eighteenth Conference of the National Committee on Art Education at the Museum of Modern Art, New York, May 5, 1960.

The title meant everything when I was up in the country, snow on the ground, and it was lonesome, and I said, "Yes, I will, sounds like a good idea, I can get down to New York." The title was inconclusive enough, would cover anything I could think of. I made some notes, came to New York. After several days I was working very seriously. I must have had twenty sheets of yellow paper in longhand. It seemed reasonably good so I got a stenographer and had it typed up. Then, as I sat reading it, I thought it was pompous, and it was didactic, and it was all the things I declaim against. I got discouraged and threw the speech away, so I have no address.

The night before last a couple of friends dropped over—Robert Motherwell and his wife, Helen Frankenthaler. Mr. Motherwell has been on the staff of Hunter College and has lectured at a number of universities. I told him my plight, and he said, "Be honest. If you are really honest, what would you say?" I said that is a very hard thing to be, and it is a very hard thing to ask other people to be, and this can only be hypothetical as if it took place in a vacuum. And if it took place in a vacuum and I were really honest with you I would apologize because I have not done better, because I have wasted time. I know that more than anybody else. I have fallen for divertissements, followed blind alleys when I should have been working. Work has always given me back more than anyone or anything so I'm not sure what I'm going to say.

In our talk Motherwell was saying, "What are your resentments?" I said, "I have a lot of resentments." And he said, "Why don't you start with those?" I want to start with some resentments. They begin early. I'll start with the first college I attended, my first hope. I resent their art without painting. I don't think I'd seen a genuine oil painting, I had not seen an original sculpture, when I went there to study. They had me making tile designs in the Department of Education. I was not able to enroll in the department which they call Fine Arts until a year or so after I had made tile designs. I had never seen a tile design in my life and I didn't know what I was doing, and neither did the college, except that they were teaching me how to teach something I couldn't do. I've been sore at art education ever since. There are a lot of things I wish people had taught me. I wish somebody had taught me to draw in proportion to my own size, to draw as freely and as easily, with the same movements that I dressed myself with, or that I ate with, or worked with in the factory. Instead, I was required to use a little brush, a little pencil, to work on a little area, which put me into a position of knitting— not exactly my forte. There wasn't a movement in my life up until that time that ever made me knit or make a tile design. I think that the first thing that I should have been taught was to work on great big paper, big sizes to utilize my natural movements toward what we will call art. It doesn't matter what it might look like. I think the freedom of gesture and the courage to act are more important than trying to make a design.

I've tried to make up for that in my teaching of other people. That has been one reason I've taught. That, and the necessity of earning a living. In the thirties my work was small—even small work was difficult to produce—so were paintings small. Part of it was the tradition of our time. I think everyone worked small—because it wouldn't fit into apartments, or because you didn't have the idea of working to your own size. Also during the WPA, at twenty-three to twenty-seven dollars a week you couldn't buy materials to make sculpture very big, and painters couldn't make paintings very big either.

As far as a way of working, my concept developed in a strange way. When I worked with parts to the whole—it was a "natural" that started in the thirties—the unities and the parts that I put together were on the defensive. Maybe I didn't mention it then, and possibly nobody knew it until the whole conception was presented, but sometimes some of those things had to be done because I didn't have the money to do it any other way. There were very few of us that made bronze castings in the thirties. Then there was a period after that of maybe ten years when one just kept working, and nothing publicly happened: little chance to show, surviving on the appreciation of friends, but mainly other artists. In the thirties it was very nice because everybody said what art was, except artists. The authorities all declaimed and in unity declared the abstract concept dead. I read it in the press any number of times. Connoisseurs and distinguished critics came from Europe declaring that our concept was dead in Europe. Presumably, so were we. The critics said so, the dealers said so—there were very few exhibitions of abstract art during those years. It seemed then that there was a known secret about art, known to the connoisseurs or the authorities. One secret about art, of course, it was all made in Europe, but then abstract concepts were also supposed to have passed. I know that it really didn't matter very much what the concept was. We all know it now. It doesn't matter so much what the point of view is, whether it is abstract or not abstract. The art that's produced depends much more on the conviction of the man who produces it. You work from your identity—that demand from yourself —and by personal conviction of your own cause more than the fads or the order of your time. I appreciate at the same time artists like Bonnard, Matisse, Picasso, Mondrian, and Kandinsky. From this group it is more the man and his challenge and how he identifies himself as an artist.

Another resentment I hold against higher education called colleges is that the teaching of tradition always left me feeling defeated. Art history has been a pre-defeat on the artist, in a contemporary sense. If I could choose I would teach the student for at least three or four years to be a painter and sculptor, and nothing else. I would teach these as the true arts. I would teach this without history or crafts.

There is no true art history, no true appreciation. All are prejudices to be developed after the teaching of painting and sculpture. If at all. They really belong to the non-artist. At this particular time in the world, I think we are ready to openly face the fact that we need painters and sculptors in society. The statement is axiomatic, probably, because they already exist. I think we should face true art and teach it. Is it practical? I imagine there are more painters and sculptors surviving today than there are potters, bookbinders, and any of the crafts. Practi-

David Smith

cally, true art teaching can hardly be objected to, but spiritually it involves an effort to teach perception—an opening toward perceptual vision, which exists nowhere else in the educational system.

I wish to make a very arbitrary statement about what art is. Art is painting and sculpture. From these we must start. It is very necessary to have a good gallery and a responsible staff and an acquisition policy to maintain the contemporary review. You cannot organize good exhibitions unless you make acquisitions. It's a stimulation to have a gallery. You teach art—painting and sculpture—more by visual stimulation than by word wisdom. I don't think that you can use half-ancient analogies in teaching painting and sculpture. I don't think you can say, in the fifteenth century such and such. Those analogies have no basis. I haven't heard one without holes. The only analogy to teach with is in the contemporary sense, or a contemporary act. You first of all teach people to use their own senses. That is not always easy. I don't know how you teach roots—visual thinking, courage, perception—but all people have and use these and do not exist without them. They develop by work and work discipline. Very few people think with words, never the artist. If you don't confuse with word thinking, the students naturally think or perceive by vision, and their evaluations are all done in a perceptual way. But much of the educational system confuses thinking, thinking by words. I've read discussions by mathematicians on the way they think. They do not think with words. Once in a while one of them does. But it may be one in about twenty. Most mathematicians think very much like artists. Their original impulses are visual.

I would like art to be taught as artists are taught and as artists make art. That is in a perceptual-visual way. In teaching art I haven't inquired who is, or who is not, going to be an artist. I don't want to teach a special art for the education department. I am interested in teaching art to the best of my ability. I do not wish to make adaptations. First of all I don't think you can be a good art teacher unless you are a good artist. I think art teachers ought to be painters or sculptors, and I think they ought to be active. They stimulate by the fact of their being. There is so much to be conveyed that is not a word matter in teaching, it is not all direction, and it is not the still life you set up. It's a stimulation, in a fine sense, a professionalism that is projected. I do maintain that the best way to learn is to follow the act with complete conviction—to teach art as though everyone in that class is going to be an artist, although we do not expect everyone to be an artist. What they do will be their own problem. And I think most artists might agree that that is the way to teach art.

We have all let anthropologists, philosophers, historians, connoisseurs and mercenaries, and everybody else tell us what art is or what it should be. But I think we ought to very simply let it be what artists say it is. And what artists say it is, you can see by their work. I would like to leave it just like that.

I use the term drive because I think it an essential element in arriving. When a student fails to do his assignment and gives an excuse instead, after two excuses I just assign a hundred extra drawings—that's a new requirement of the course for them before they can pass. That's not so bad. I've seen dullards, after they did a hundred drawings under pressure, get so they liked to draw. One of the best students I had was a girl to whom I once gave this assignment. Of course, we may have had to decide what was a drawing. I accepted the definition of drawing as any piece of paper that had a mark on it, on the basis of self-respect. A student wouldn't give you a hundred pieces of paper with a mark on each one. Possibly one sheet of paper with one mark, but it isn't long before he feels the need of more than one mark. By the time students make three or four marks they are already draftsmen. Everybody is intimidated about marks on paper, or marks on canvas. One is a very simple thing to do. You must help to uninhibit and unintimidate people before they can get involved in the creative act. I think that is one of the important things in teaching—to unintimidate. Freedom should be first before judgment and self-criticism.

Utilizing another atmosphere is often an elevating aid in drawing. Music appeals to me in that way, rather than art history or art appreciation. I would much rather teach with music. I would also prefer to have them read the autobiography of Sean O'Casey to learn about conflict. Practically nobody I know has so much conflict, or meets so much opposition, as O'Casey did in his early life. Even now, up to today, O'Casey's life isn't without it. He has high respect, but he's not a man of means. The first year is very important to make students work. Because our whole attitude is too soft, I am against students wasting my time and their opportunity—it leads to the wrong life-attitudes. To develop the work pattern, you may have to drive, but work in the class should be tougher than usually it is in most schools. It's just as important to develop drive as it is to develop the coordination of movement of your daily action to the coordination of making art. I wouldn't remove art from the movement of the person. As I said at the outset, people have different states of gesture. Some people move bigger than others. I would try to develop the gestures so that the act of growing came within the natural gesture of that person until he is free, and until his decision controlled him to do otherwise. I said art ought to be taught by working artists. I am certain of it. I think the whole order of teaching should be toward developing the student to the highest degree. I

David Smith

don't think direction without example is effective. Poor teaching is not always the teacher's fault. But everything is the teacher's fault. If you really started on it, you would probably have to change the president, the board of trustees, and the deans and all that sort of thing to get a decent teaching situation to produce the best students. Ossification has started at the top.

There is an illusive quality called determination. I don't know how you teach determination. Sometimes the most able and the most brilliant students are the ones who fall out before they arrive at a career. On the other hand, I've seen seemingly dull students succeed because of their determination. I've seen it happen a number of times. I've witnessed it recently, under my teaching. Seemingly I could get nothing across—no response to urgency. They were slow on the take, or they needed other people, or they needed other experience. But finally, not being the best artists, being the slowest and showing the least result, they turned out to have the bite—maybe they were bitten harder. And because they got there they had to work harder. I know two or three artists in New York who came out of the Midwest. They were not exceptional to start, but they are now. It took longer.

In teaching there are statements from other arts that complement our own direction. There are statements by Camus, Stravinsky, O'Casey —there are statements by Gabo, Ben Shahn, Duchamp. There are hundreds of statements by artists. You can even take the difference of position in statements by Kokoschka and Shahn as against maybe Duchamp or Gabo—even in different points of view. But those things have so much more contemporary and immediate importance for the young artist than Plotinus or Theophilus or Vitruvius or most anybody of the classic position, because I do not believe that artists utilize the myth of history and the past. I think the most impressive and the most useful thing they get is that their true influence comes from the present: it's very immediate, it's very much like a family, it's very much like their own family—father, grandfather. This particular position in time is quite twentieth century. I don't think the influence of the Renaissance—I don't care how much Renaissance you inject, or how much Gothic or Romanesque or Greek or Roman you present—helps in a working direction like the feeling of their own family, like immediacy and the heritage of their own time.

You work as you feel—and you are as you are. You come from your own family—your own heritage—and that is a thing you cannot denounce. You also exist in life within that family, and within that century, and within that time. I don't think you ever leave that, no matter how much or how nobly you aspire, or how many ancient ideas you embrace.

I'm not much given to art history for students. I think the contemporary position of this student is more important than all the art history you can give him.

O'Casey said, "Thrust ahead slowly and deeply—if it is in you to do a thing. If you decide that you can, then do it even if it keeps you busy until the very last hour of your life." I would have liked somebody to have told me that when I went to college. I didn't know it was that easy. I didn't know it could be done at all.

Somehow it seems to me that the way you progress is by the amount of conflict and the amount of struggle that you survive. That also means the physical struggle. The more of the conflicts you survive, the stronger you are for the next one. It happens in daily life. To any creative person it happens every day in his work. It's a natural thing in working. But the strength is not the high-flown ideology. It is the conviction you have in yourself, how you identify yourself as the artist, as the worker. You never teach equality. To my way of thinking equality is defeatist. You have to teach him what the world is now. The challenge is to excel beyond what he is given. The artist-student has to be different and better than his history. Any type of equality teaching is only in a sense historic teaching, because you are leading the students up to the unknown quantity which becomes his challenge. You can help identify him in the time he lives, and with his family. That is why I say equality is defeatist. The challenge is beyond the known factor of equality.

I would also teach this hypothetical student that provincialism or coarseness or unculture is greater for creating art than finesse and polish. Creative art has a better chance of developing from coarseness and courage than from culture. One of the good things about American art is that it doesn't have the spit-and-polish that some foreign art has. It is coarse. One of its virtues is coarseness. A virtue can be anything, as long as that conviction projects an origin—and fresh courage. As long as it has the fire, I don't think it matters, because there are all kinds of qualities in art, and I'm not very involved in the differentiation or the qualitative value of who has what in art. I would much rather have a man who has no ideals in art, but who has tremendous drive about it with the fire to make it.

There are minor things that relate to our time now that are changing. I am personally interested in a man-made object. Now because this is a productive age and it is more unique, there is freshness of origin. If I'm making a sculpture I wish to have just as much integrity as a painter. I want to make one image, I want to have controlled every make in it. I am not the least bit interested in having one image and having it cast into reproductions. In this relation I think very often about the flood of Degas sculptures. There were Degas waxes, small ones. Now they are

154   David Smith

reproduced by the foundry—there's a fair amount of myth and misinformation about it—but they are not originals, they are reproductions. They never had the eye of the artist on them. He had his eye on the original piece. The waxes were later restored and now seem to exist in the hundreds. I would, rather than see all these thousands of Degas horses running loose, make a trip to the original waxes and see the touch of the artist's hand. In the thirties there was a great deal of talk about art for the people. The idea seemed to be that you make art and spread it out to a lot of different people. I think that people should spread themselves and go to the museum where the art is.

I am looking at some photographs which you needn't see, because I'm using them to refer to the way I work. Very often, I seem to be much more concerned with the monsters than with what are called beauties. But these monsters are big constructions which have wheels. Sometimes the wheels work and sometimes not. But the wheels have meaning, they are no more functional than wheels on an Indian stone temple. It is a playful idea projecting movement. I don't feel at all like the age of graces. I like girls, but I don't feel like using that feminine grace in concepts. The equality has worked it in. I don't think this is the age of grace. I don't know whether my monsters on wheels will become graces to other people and I don't know whether or not they will be rationalized as being a need or a statement of my time. They are non-rational, but they filled a need within me. If I try to tell how I make art, it seems difficult. There is no order in it. A night or two ago I had stopped to see Mike Kanemitsu. In talking, Mike had mentioned Zadkine and Paris. The reference to Zadkine and my train of thought going back made me remember about a big sculpture I wanted to make. So I might never have thought of that one if he hadn't mentioned Zadkine and if I hadn't thought of concave and convex, and if I hadn't thought of that sculpture, which I had finished and which had already been shipped to the West Coast, that I probably will not see again. I wouldn't have made the sculpture I am going to make this summer which is going to be made out of big forms, but that's the way process can go. I'm trying to explain that I have no noble thought process or concept. Its origin is often chance. Yet of all the things I was thinking in those certain moments that we were sitting—I guess it was an hour—while talking and drinking beer, I thought of a hundred other relationships, but none of them fitted in my niche.

I spoke about the integrity of painters. For example, a painter makes a picture. Even if he could sell two or three, or five or seven, he would not consider reproducing—but the practice still exists in sculpture. Maybe a sculptor will make from one to nine or any of those numbers. Each cast shrinks from the original as the metal cools, and the bronze undergoes changes. There's welding, grinding, and manufacturing on it that is not of the artist's hand. It doesn't come out with the same integrity that a painter presents in a picture. Nobody can make a copy with integrity. A painter couldn't make a copy or have a copy made with the integrity he used in the original picture. I just want to see sculpture reach that state of integrity, too. I admit that right now it's pretty much up to the individual sculptor.

Gauguin made a little terra-cotta, and there are now ten bronzes of terra-cottas. And he didn't mean to make the bronzes, any more than Daumier made bronzes. Somebody gets a bronze from a little Daumier wax, and somebody else makes a number of bronzes from this bronze, and bronzes get made because they have a royal establishment that true art belongs in bronze—it may have once been royal demand and designation, and it still seems to be going that way. Some day people will understand that the original gesture of the artist—the original object—is the true art, that the others are the reproductions. And I think that soon the original plaster sculpture will be truer art than the bronze is in the minds of artists, as it will have to be in the minds of museum directors and the public. Reproductions must be only reproductions. The authorities involved, and the historians and critics, have not spoken about this very much. They haven't very loudly proclaimed what are the true bronzes, or what is true art—not as loud as they should. Nor do there seem to be any laws or rules about it. But I would like to see it recognized. That's it.

Report on Voltri

The following notes concern David Smith's work in Voltri, Italy, in 1962.

Italsider

Ilva, in Voltri, where the wild strawberries grow, was a complex of some five factories set in a narrow valley, based by a small stream, once making springs, trucks, parts for flatcars, bolts, spikes, balls, many things by forging. It had been consumed by the automation of Italsider at Cornegliano halfway in toward Genoa eight kilometers distant.

As the guest of Italsider I lived at the Columbia Exelsior Hotel in Genoa, was picked up at 6:30 by my Italsider car, stopped for Ruello my interpreter, arrived at the machine shop where we started work as the sun came over the hill and hit the shop door. For the first ten days Lynn Chadwick lived at the same hotel, so we rode together and kept the same schedule, 6:30 to 6:30. Chadwick worked at Cornegliano; some days I'd ask the chauffeur to pick me up and go to Cornegliano for lunch with Chadwick, for on the top of a hill above the factory was a home-style restaurant, with the best local cooking to be found. Italsider had arranged my lunches in a shore restaurant supplied by local fishermen each day. Chadwick came to Voltri for the seafood, wild strawberries, apricots, fungi, etc. Food may not make art—but without any outside life, it helps. I can take it good or frugally—but when one lives alone in the hills it's a treat. And in a restaurant one doesn't have to wash the dishes.

A few times we were joined by our Italsider contacts whose interest was to see that we were happy and had what we needed.

Although Menotti had said I had the red carpet and I had asked for a big-chested interpreter, I was fortunate in finding Sig. Ruello who had been a POW in New Mexico and was an expediter of supplies at Cornegliano. He kept oxygen acetylene, polishing equipment, acids, safety equipment, etc., coming in as needed. Everything was supplied; I took nothing but my safety shoes and glasses.

Beginning

The first Sunday alone in these factories—functional in an era long past, abandoned only a few months—were like Sundays in Brooklyn in 1934 at the Terminal Iron Works, except that here I could use anything I found, dragging parts between buildings to find their new identity. I thought of my Agricolas. There was a similarity—but the language was different—and the size bolder.

The first two Sundays—not even a skeleton crew around—the great quiet of stopped machines—the awe, the pull, exceeded that of visits to museums in Genoa or even the ancient art in other cities. Part is personal heritage, part prejudice against connoisseurs' castles. Since I've had identity, the desire to create excels over the desire to visit.

There is something quite middle class about ancient art in museums —choices by the order of scribes, fakes, and gifts, and rationalized purchases mix to one part with ninty-nine parts destroyed or still uncovered.

My preference is ethnographic and archaeological, where discovery was made without taste, where bargains and whims of guilt-ridden iconoclasts' bronze-plate attributions are less in evidence. There are no sedan chairs in an old factory.

Forge

The beauties of the forge shop, parts dropped partly forged, cooled now but stopped in progress—as if the human factor had dissolved and the great dust settled—the found tombs of early twentieth century, from giants to tweezers headed for the open hearth to feed the world's speediest rolls.

Archaeologists have their iron interests back 5,000 years. In the yard where iron has lain shedding scale and scrap, punchings scraps from shearing, I found parts of my nature not over seventy years old in the first inch, but this flat beside a stream near the sea may, farther down, hold museum iron. I brought back to Bolton handfuls of findings for no greater reason than that they fit with my miscellany and complement the manhole cover from Brooklyn which hangs on my wall. The archaeologists may go as far as L. S. B. Leakey and fill many halls, but my vision is in dreaming the host of events destroyed in their time. It is possible the museums are too small in truth to form historianisms.

Blacksmith Shop

Speciality tongs were hand-forged at stations. Since this method was abandoned, the work in process was left in varying stages of finish. At this blacksmith station I worked up units but no completion. I shipped the units to Bolton, where part are in the Voltri-Bolton series of December, 1962, and January, 1963.

Layout Table

A thick steel layout table was never white. I had it painted with lime and water. Ancient in use, practical because it was there, it gave me an order contact which from then on let me work freely without order. The gauges and calipers were those of blacksmiths, rough and imprecise. After *Voltri XXII,* five pieces of a different scale came from the layout table. One owned by Carandente, one my daughters gave Menotti, and an iron ballet dancer for Mike Pepper's daughter Jori, a devoted doll collector. Some of the units and gauge assemblies conceived in Voltri were shipped back and figured in spray paintings, producing a white sculptural image against a dark ground. These are in technique like the paintings in the French & Company [gallery] show of 1959.

Yard

The yards had flowers and fig trees planted by yard workers. Now deserted by automation, these factories were from the handmade days, the 10-11-12 hour days when working was living. In the new automated

David Smith

plant, the hours are shorter, the man is a machine part. He lives outside the gates only. One remaining symbol not common to our factories is the wine bottle—and an aluminum pasta container held hot by the company steam table. Their yard had the locale and nostalgia of my first ironworks of 1934 in Brooklyn, except on a grand scale, and here what hung or was to be found was mine.

Plates of varying weights lay rusting in the yard. I used them, but I had to hurry. A salvage crew was in several days a week with their gondolas and switch engine for heavy scrap to feed the melt at Corne-gliano. Had I failed to take it first, I could have gone to the mill and got it new, but I felt opportunity and time even shorter than in Bolton. I can work against time for myself like I cannot work for a commission.

Workbenches

A factory stripped of its function—leaves on the floor from holes in the roof—quiet except for a bird cheep. From factory to factory I laid out workbenches—I finished two there, left more. I felt the awe and the scared air—like one returning survivor after holocaust, and as I had felt, very young in Decatur, when I went through the window in my first abandoned factory. After the first shock of its immensity and the privilege, I felt at home, and then to work.

Mill

What I found I could use, what I arranged was never touched by any of the occasional directors checking the dismantling or the salvage crew —even those assemblies unmarked. In the big operating factory at Cornegliano any plate end or found piece I wrote my name on and "Voltri" was delivered. I had been introduced by Sig. Piccardo and had full freedom of the mill and scrap cars. Anything I didn't find I asked for.

Workmen

Variera, the machine shop foreman, was the champion snail finder. The snails were always north on the compass end of his umbrella. He was a magician in producing supplies—he knew about every stock item left behind. Vassallo and Ferrando were welders and cutters first class— they could do any operation with the most primitive equipment. Both had once used the welding machines, so ancient, so big, the company had not bothered to move them. One D.C. transformer must have been the first ever made. Ruello had spent several years in our Southwest in a POW camp. He was my interpreter, communicator for telephone messages, expediter, and white-collar liaison. When not involved, he worked. Through him we all communicated about religion, family, politics, customs, desires. My men were about equally divided politically between communism and socialism. All living in a small community within sight of the factory, they had political ease in association, with no obvious problems in relationship to work. I was at ease with them all. I've always moved through the climate of workmen more evenly than through that of the connoisseurs.

Coffee break was in the morning, but wine break and delicacies were at 3 P.M. Each man was a wine maker, and sampling of homemade wine was a contribution which brought forth chiding and good-natured devaluing of the others' wine. Cova the electrician was a bird man—he could hear the chirp of a newborn bird in the highest peak. We had whole birds sautéed in oil and garlic. We had mussels, roasted on a flat steel sheet until they opened, from Cova. We had snails found in the yard in the green of the tracks by foreman Variera, who poked for them with his umbrella, after their twenty-one days' confinement of course. Special snail roasting by Mother, a specialist. I took my crew for lunches, which I intended to pay for but found that I could not; Italsider had figured it all in. I left my noontime restaurant and my Genoa hotel unable to pay; being their guest was complete.

Problem

Day 1 to be introduced in white collar to my workmen, to whom I couldn't speak—awkward to us both. In equal garb the next day. Request for swept floor not met. I swept floor. Request for moving of heavy objects not moved exact place. I moved to positions. After welding, moving, sweeping, my collar was O.K. We worked together from then on great. An interpreter and unknown work added to the first problems, but for only several days—we understood, and their desire to produce first class and to my need never failed.

Concentration

My own problems surmount the practical—to what degree of abstraction in concentration can one delve with noise and workmen who present other presences.

My thoughts were often in creative vision during factory work. I've put in years at machines—dreaming aesthetic ends—one never becomes oblivious to the surrounding order—in concentrated work alone under ideal conditions—outside vistas intrude like sex—hungers and assorted fears, fear in survival—lonesomeness for my children—many waves intrude during the most ideal setup. One works with one's nature—sets

David Smith

his own equilibrium, develops his resources, evens up his rage in whatever conditions present or the first hundred works would not have been set.

When elements like noise, others, dirt, grease enter the procedure, they are but elements in nature more easily transposed than intruding mental pops.

Safety measures—machines—like any other conflict, can be consumed and utilized toward complete concentration as any other conflict which one trips over.

Dream

A dream is a dream never lost. I've had it inside a 4-8-4 on the top of a Diesel engine, they have been in a size dream. I found an old flatcar, asked for, and was given it. Had I used the flatcar for the base and made a sculpture on the top, the dream would have been closer.

I could have loaded a flatcar with vertical sheets, inclined planes, uprights with holes, horizontals supported—

I could have made a car with the nude bodies of machines, undressed of their details and teeth—

I could have made a flatcar with a hundred anvils of varying sizes and character which I found at forge stations.

I could have made a flatcar with painted skeletal wooden patterns.

In a year I could have made a train. The flatcar I had is now melted in the open hearth and rolled into sheet. The beauty of the ballet of a white-to-red-to-black sheet in a fast-rolling mill at different speeds running back and forth billowing steam with the quenches is a memory for me of automation fed by my flatcar.

The trucks were too old for the tracks, it was quite antique—despite the offer to put this flat on a modern flat for transport to Spoleto—the tunnels along the coast ruled out height for the work. The closest to realization came when Mulas chose to put finished work on the flat for his photos. So many dreams have been lost to lack of material, workspace, storage, etc., that one more becomes another wish.

Unit of Six was *Voltri I*—it came desperately—the first piece to unify after gathering plates, pieces, trimmings, from the big mill and moving all to the solitude and emptiness of the Voltri factories. Starting, it began to move other works until two, three, four were in progress. *Voltri II* finished May 26 and shipped to Spoleto June 6 with Chadwick's big black-and-yellow structures. This piece probably carried in my consciousness from Bolton since I had been working cube unities since 1955. I had gone to Genoa expecting to make stainless pieces, but Italsider had not yet put into operation its new stainless mill in the south. There were Italsider mills throughout Italy and I had my choice. The next question to Menotti after agreeing to go was which of the cities do you like best—his answer of Genoa decided me. I've never regretted it —it was the best work period I've had.

Voltri II, IV, V, IX, XI, XIV, XV, XVII all have an element in their structure which I'll call a chopped cloud, although in different relationships the visual response varies. When a billet rolls out to a sheet no two ends are the same, as in the edges of clouds. There is great wonder and a beauty of natural growth in these variations. I cut off many ends and flew them many ways. I would like a hundred more. I have never before seen or possessed chopped-iron cloud ends. There are ends on a table. An end on a full cloud. Ends caught on a tower. Ends in a tower. Pennant ends on circles. And ends making a whole. In the mountains, clouds are in my daily unconsciousness, but I've never had one before.

Voltri VIII. When a sheet runs back and forth under the rolls, before it shoots through quench and to the next rolling reduction, a rarity can happen—it can stub a toe, instead of running, fold up like a great stick of gum. I saw one, sent it to Voltri, watched it in many positions until I found its relationship.

Voltri III was called the little old lady by one of my workmen. It was placed high on the last tier of the reconstructed part of the Roman theater of Spoleto. There had been no plans to use the theater this year. It was an emergency measure by Director Carandente in a desire to use all my work, and a most fortunate event for my work. A more beautiful setting I could not conceive. Here I put my work in the fields. That was an emergency, lacking storage space. I did not conceive a field complex, but since it grew of necessity I accept it.

Voltri VI, VII, XIII. Forgings too big for hand—worked by drop hammers—are transported from ovens to hammer by a tong which is a chariot on two wheels pushed by men. Three remained which I remade for carrying and being a part of, in *Voltri VI, Voltri VII, Voltri VIII*.

Circles have long been a preoccupation, more primary than squares. Wheels are circles with mobility, from the first wheel of man to wheels on Indian stone temples, to a target on a pyramid I painted in 1934, to all the suns and poetic imagery of movement, to the practical fact that my sculpture is getting too big to move without built-in rolling. Horse chariots are not in my picture.

Voltri VI is a tong with wheels and two end clouds. One cloud rests in the spoon—each cloud end goes up from the tongue unsupported.

Voltri VII is a chariot ram with five bar forgings. They are not personages—they are forgings.

Voltri XIII is a circus wheel chariot with the spoon turned over, a solid guitar forging with a punched hole—with cloud parts below and above its tongue.

Voltri XI started from a tong head demanding a thick, oval, curved, supplicated hood held up by a vertical. It started in the fly ash of the floor; it never changed from the first few minutes of seeing. I could have worked a year and made a hundred. I had others underway. The final day I piled parts and all the tongs I wanted—the safety signs which now are on the walls in Bolton—and asked for the lot to be shipped to the U.S.

Voltri XX was the only piece finished of what I thought would be ten or twelve using tongs. The shipment of tongs has figured in twenty-two pieces made here. The series still continues.

Voltri X was painted with red lead, but all the rest were cured with phosphoric acid, washed, and lacquered.

Voltri XXI, a chair, the damnedest chair I've ever seen, made of angle irons and scrap, the hardest most unfunctional overweight chair possible, was up-ended in a corner of the second floor of the spring shop. I saw it the first day at Voltri—I took it and looked at it every day of my time there—I made parts—and rejected them—I sat pieces and ideas on it. We worried each other throughout my other work. Close to my final day, parts from pieces, parts unused, came up and placed themselves, but the chair that could have held up elephants lost its identity, and finished up so challenging that there will be other chair sculptures sometime.

Cubi IX, shown in the lower part of Spoleto in front of a fourteenth-century church, built with Roman blocks and seventeenth-century restorations, might seem odd in description, but looked fine. Professor Carandente had an innate feeling for mounting and choosing sites. The most diverse sculpture related, as if it belonged in all styles of architecture. *Cubi IX* was made in Bolton and shipped to Spoleto before I had agreed to go there. Its height of 107⅜ inches was elevated on a six-foot pillar of tufa blocks bound in iron bands giving an over-all height of about fifteen feet. Its stainless cubes in a different way held with the soft variables of the church wall stones.

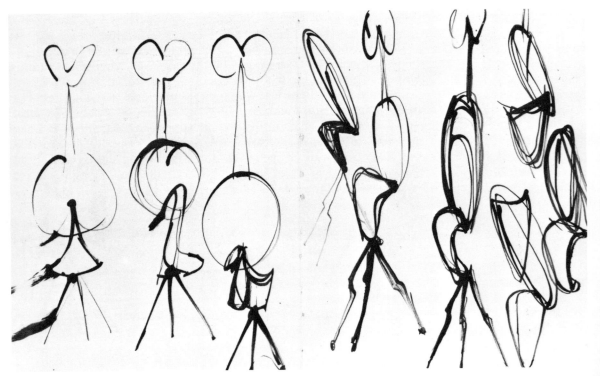

Preliminary sketches for *Tanktotem III*, in a notebook of c. 1950–54.

||| interviews

Interview   *David Sylvester*

The following tape-recorded discussion with David Smith took place in New York on June 16, 1961, and was conducted by David Sylvester of the British Broadcasting Corporation. It was published in Living Arts *in April, 1964.*

David Smith: There is no collaboration nor is there any affinity between [architects and artists]. Architects have had the opinion that they are the fathers of all the arts, that their buildings are sculptures, and that the use of painting and sculpture ofttimes defiles their purities. There are no affinities between us, especially with me. I do not solicit architects. I have seen that man works better when he is working within his own spirit than when he is working with the domination or the collaboration of the architect. Now we're not working for money. We're working to make greater art out of ourselves. We're working to extend our own potential. I don't think any of us really wish to revert and repeat a point of arrival that we've arrived at before to make a repeat for the sake of money. I don't know where this idea of collaboration would be. Mostly architects look down upon us, and mostly architects are big businessmen here and we're just one of their small clients in the building. They choose to put the marble in the men's room and they put the bronze in the fixtures and they really don't need sculpture at all.

David Sylvester: *If you knew an architect whom you found sympathetic, would you like to see some of your sculpture placed in an architectural setting outside buildings? Inside the large entries of buildings?*

I would like to see it, certainly, but I'm working in quite a large size, you know. My work is running from nine to fifteen feet high. Right now I have a very modest acceptance and rather small amount of sales, and I am surviving without architects. And if they choose to use my work as it stands I would be delighted to sell it to them and have them use it, but I do not think that I will change my point of view to meet theirs. I have no natural affinity with modern architecture. I can't afford to live in any of these buildings. It's no part of my world. My sculpture is part of my world; it's part of my everyday living; it reflects my studio, my house, my trees, the nature of the world I live in. And the nature of the world that painters and sculptors live in is walkup places with cracks; you look out the windows and see chimney tops, and I don't think any of us can make the old-fashioned royal bow to suit their needs. Liberty, or freedom of our position, is the greatest thing we've got.

There's a picture in London of the American artist of your genera-

tion, you and the action painters, of being rather a group. Has there been a sort of collaboration of ideas between you? And did you find knowing Pollock, being a close friend of Pollock and people like that, fruitful for your work?

No. We talked about other things usually. But we did spring from the same roots and we had so much in common and our parentage was so much the same that, like brothers, we didn't need to.

The parentage, I suppose, of course, was the whole Cubist thing. But why do you think it suddenly exploded in this way into this terrific growth that began in the late forties of American art?

Well, Pollock, de Kooning, and practically everybody I can think of who is forty to fifty now and sort of "arrived" artists, in a sense—they all came from a depression time. We all came from the bond of the WPA, which we affectionately call it; it was the Works Progress Administration and it was a government employment of artists for . . .

The New Deal thing?

Yes, it was definitely the New Deal thing, and somewhat of a defensive thing. We made very little more by working than people drew for not working for unemployed relief. We drew maybe five or six dollars a week more for working . . .

Yes.

. . . which was very nice because for the first time, collectively, we belonged somewhere.

And this gave you a stimulus?

Well, we belonged to society that way. It gave us unity, it gave us friendship, and it gave us a collective defensiveness.

You mean belonging to society at large or merely belonging to your own group?

In a sense we belonged to society at large. It was the first time we ever belonged or had recognition from our own government that we existed.

Do you still feel that you belong in that way or has that now been lost?

Well, the government doesn't belong—we don't belong to the government any more; I mean times have changed.

Do you still get any patronage?

No patronage, not that I know of. A few of our more traditional men have had monument patronages or they design a coin or something like that, but there is no patronage generally speaking, and not even recognition.

So the postwar thing owed absolutely nothing to any help from officialdom?

We owe nothing to the federal government for recognition, no. Not now.

There wasn't a lot of help at first from American collectors, was there —the private collectors?

Private collectors were quite few and far between. But there was another thing the WPA did. It stimulated the interest in art; you see, while some artists were employed, don't forget there were a lot of teachers, and there were critics and all people related to the arts. There were many public classes, adult painting classes, adult sculpture classes, WPA exhibitions that traveled throughout the country; they went to union halls and schools and places like that where art had never been shown before. And there was an interest stimulated there by people, and the response to it, and also other people to do it. You know, amateur response is sort of groundwork for professional collectors. Most collectors can paint or draw to a degree, and so therefore they seem to recognize the artists who are full-time artists quicker.

So really, government help in the thirties had a lot to do with creating the climate which produced this postwar thing, although there hasn't been subsequent help?

Yes—reasons are very hard to find, and reasons are never one thing, they are a hundred things—I can't think of one thing that stimulated the response of the public better than the WPA educational projects did. Nor do I know anything that kept so many artists alive during the thirties than the WPA. There was nothing else.

A lot of the work that was being done in the thirties by the present abstract painters was sort of figurative work, some form of social realism, wasn't it? Some connection with Diego Rivera and so on?

The great body of work at that time was called social realism which did relate to Rivera and using figures.

But not in your own case?

Not in our own case. Many of those men who were what were called nonobjectivists went right through the thirties firmly convinced of their own stand; there were many of us—not too many—who came from fathers or grandfathers who were Cubists. We came not very directly, you see; we came through the French magazine *Transition* and through *Cahiers d'Art*. We came through both of those magazines, and we came through men like Stuart Davis, and Jean Xceron, and John Graham, and men like that who more or less went back and forth between Paris and here and told us what was going on in Europe.

You yourself were working abstract before a lot of the painters, weren't you?

I have been essentially an abstract sculptor.

But weren't you in Europe yourself for some time in the late thirties?

In 1935 and '36. Most of us tried to go to Europe if we could; most of us did. Of course, de Kooning had come from Europe . . .

Quite.

And Gorky had come from Europe. Graham was a Russian, and he had come from Europe. Stuart Davis had gone to Europe earlier.

How do you feel it affected your development—going there at that moment?

It was very important. Most of all, it was one of the greatest points of my own liberation mentally. You see, before—in the early part of the thirties—we all were working for a kind of utopian position, or at least a position where somebody liked our work. In the early thirties none of us—like Pollock or Gorky or de Kooning—could really, none of us could show our work any place, nobody wanted to show it, and it seemed that the solution was to be expatriates. Most of the men a little older than we were had seen the solution in expatriatism all the way from Mallorca to Paris itself. And the one thing that I learned in 1935 and '36—I was in England and Russia and Greece and France and places like that—and the one thing when I came back that I realized was that I belonged here; my materials were here, my thoughts were here, my birth was here, and whatever I could do had to be done here. I thoroughly gave up any idea of ever being an expatriate. So I laid into work very hard. That must have been in the minds of other men. Otherwise, there wouldn't be so many of us here now.

It's often said that one of the reasons why American art built up after the war was that it was stimulated by European artists who came here from Paris in 1940 and stayed here during the war. Do you think there is anything in that or not?

That is part of the scene and it is important. It has been very rewarding to us to have men like Lipchitz, and Mondrian, and Gabo become Americans and live here with us; that is good and it's been very nice. We have met them and we have found that they were humans like we were and they were not gods and they were fine artists. And so we know more about the world now.

In the thirties, of course, a lot of the more or less social realist work that was being done then was involved in social commitment. I believe you were exceptional in having a strong left-wing commitment but working abstract.

I have strong social feelings. I do now. And about the only time I was ever able to express them in my work was when I made a series of medallions which were against the perils or evils of war, against inhuman things. They were called *Medals for Dishonor*. When I was in the British Museum in London in 1936 I bought a series of postcards

David Smith

which were made during the First World War, and they were war medallions of the Germans. And that, and Sumerian cylinder seals that I had been studying in Greece, and intaglio carving, and so forth, impelled me to do that series of medallions which took me three years. I first had to learn how to carve in reverse in order to make these. It was about the only thing I have ever done which contributed to a social protest. I don't feel that I have to protest with my work. Whatever society I belong to must take me for my ability; my effort is to drive to the fullest extent those few talents that were given me, and propaganda is not necessarily my forte.

I talk about your being abstract, but it isn't fair; a lot of your forms seem to me to be referential to nature. I see a lot of your big stainless steel things as personage. Are they at all this for you?

They don't start that way. But how can a man live off of his planet? How on earth can he know anything that he hasn't seen or doesn't exist in his own world? Even his visions have to be made up of what he knows, of the forms and the world that he knows. He can't go off his planet with visions no matter how they're put together. And he naturally uses his proportion and his sort of objectivity. He can't get away from it. There is no such thing as *truly* abstract. Man always has to work from his life.

You have no preconceptions about which way the thing is going to go?

I try not to have. I try to approach each thing without following the pattern that I made with the other one. They can begin with any idea. They can begin with a found object, they can begin with no object. They can begin sometimes even when I'm sweeping the floor and I stumble and kick a few parts and happen to throw them into an alignment that sets me off thinking and sets off a vision of how it would finish if it all had that kind of accidental beauty to it. I want to be like a poet, in a sense. I don't want to seek the same orders. Of course, I'm a human being, I have limited ability, and there's always an order there. People recognize my work even if I think that I've really been far out in this work. I strive very hard to move a little bit but you can't move very far. Picasso moves far. He's a great man who moves very far. But I still recognize Picasso's work no matter how far he's moved from one phase or one new picture or one new sculpture; I always recognize his work.

How would you analyze the difference between your work and its intentions and the Cubist constructions—you know, González, Picasso —of which it's a continuation?

Well, living here in America at that time, going to school at the time that I went to school, I didn't read French, so when I had a *Cahiers d'Art* I didn't know what it was about. I learned from the pictures just the same as if I were a child, in a certain sense. I learned the world from seeing before I ever learned the world from words. So my world was the Dutch movement De Stijl; it was Russian Constructivism; it was Cubism; it was even Surrealism. Or even German Expressionism. Or even Monet. All these things I did not know had divisions in them. They all fitted in to me. They were all so new and so wonderful and they all came to me at one time, practically. The historians hadn't drawn the lines yet as to which was which and where at which particular time, and my heritage was all those things simultaneously. So I am all those things, I hope, with a very strong kind of intellectual regard for Cubism and an admiration for it because it was great at a particular time. It was both painting and sculpture.

Taking Cubism, Surrealism, Expressionism, not worrying about the thing—I wonder whether the vitality of postwar American art has something to do with this sort of absolute freedom of attitude which you've talked about in yourself. I wonder whether this also applies to people like de Kooning and Pollock, and whether this has helped them not to worry but to take what they could and what they wanted to take quite freely from earlier modern art.

I think it has. Gorky didn't read French. And I don't think Bill [de Kooning] read French either. We were all together at a particular time in the early days, and we were sort of expatriates. We drank coffee together in cafeterias, and when I say we drank coffee it was usually one cup because few of us could afford more than one five-cent cup of coffee in those days, plus a cookie maybe. And all we did was walk around and talk sometimes. But mostly we worked. And we each sort of took according to what we wanted. You must remember I had come from Indiana and I had only seen a sculpture a couple of years before that, or a painting. Gorky came into Providence and de Kooning came into New York [from Europe]. I think they all had a little bit more, knowing of museums and art, than I did before, and they both were European in a sense, and I think all Europeans know more about art than people from Indiana do. I don't think I had seen a museum out in Indiana or Ohio other than some very, very dark picture with sheep in it in the public library. But I didn't know anything about art until I came to New York.

But you'd wanted to produce art before? Or this happened when you came?

I wanted to be a painter when I came.

And you did paint for some years?

I painted for some years. I've never given it up. I always—even if I'm having trouble with a sculpture—I always paint my troubles out.

What was it that made you turn from painting to sculpture suddenly?

I think it was seeing Picasso's iron sculpture in a *Cahiers d'Art* about

David Smith

1928 or 1929. Seeing iron and factory materials used in producing art was quite a revelation, and since I had worked in factories and I have known iron and metal and metalworking since I have been very young, it came to me that it should be. After my first year in college I worked on the assembly line in the Studebaker plant in South Bend, Indiana. I had seen ironwork in the Russian Constructivists — Rodchenko and Malevich and — I don't know — Tatlin. I'd seen reproductions of their work sometimes in German magazines. So it was a revelation in a way. Later on I learned that González had done the welding for Picasso on those 1928–29 works that went into 1930, but I didn't know it at the time, and if it had said so in the article it was in French and I wouldn't have known it anyhow.

This seems to be important, incidentally — going back to what we were talking about before — the fact that you and the others were seeing the works in reproduction and you weren't reading the texts and maybe this was why you were able to use them so freely.

Yes. And I also liked the idea that we have no history, that we have no art history, and we pay no attention to art historians. We all were pretty raw I think.

You weren't at all — in your use of sheet metal and so on — you weren't at all influenced by Calder?

No. I knew metalworking before I knew Calder. And Calder is one of our great men, and he is earlier by a few years than any of the rest of us. Calder had worked in Paris quite a bit in the early days, though he did go to school here in New York at the Art Students League, I have been told.

Have you ever had any temptation to work in traditional materials, carving or modeling?

I do both. I model in wax and make bronzes that way, and I carve sometimes; some of my early work was carved. I don't choose to close out any method, approach, or material. Oh, I draw. I draw figures and things like that at times.

Do you ever do it from a model? Do you ever do it from nature?

Sure. As a matter of study and a matter of balance. I draw a great deal, because sculpture is such hard work and if I put in ten hours or eleven hours a day or more at hard labor, you know, the sort of dirty work of my profession, I like to take a bath and change my clothes and spend the rest of the day drawing.

You do it all yourself, don't you? I mean you could now afford studio assistants.

I can't use studio assistants any more than Mondrian could have used assistants to paint in solid areas or any more than de Kooning or any of my friends can use somebody else to put the backgrounds in, even though they might just be pure white. They don't want the marks of another hand on their own work. Now that is twentieth century, too.

It is defensive in a certain way because it's contradictory to the progression of this age. We are among the few people left who are making the object from start to finish.

You never feel it will be conceivable for you to make a model and have an assistant make it on a big scale?

No. I don't even make copies. If I make a cast sculpture I make *one* and all the marks are mine. I don't approve of copies, and I don't make and produce copies for the sake of making more money.

And this, of course, connects you very closely to the painters of your generation, doesn't it? I mean this to-and-fro between the artist and the material, this special emphasis on it now. This makes you very closely linked with Pollock and de Kooning.

Well, we were all friends and I talked with painters and I belong with painters, in a sense, and all my early friends were painters because we all studied together. And I never conceived of myself as anything other than a painter because my work came right through the raised surface, and color and objects applied to the surface. Some of the greatest contributions of sculpture to the twentieth century are by painters. Had it not been for painters, sculpture would be in a very sorry position.

Some of the greatest departures in the concept of sculpture have been made by Picasso and Matisse. There was a series of heads that Matisse made called *Jeannette*. In there are some of the very brilliant departures in the concept of sculpture. Painting and sculpture aren't very far apart.

This is one of the great twentieth-century discoveries, isn't it?

I hope it is.

Now that a lot of you have become extremely successful and are getting big prices now, is this going to make a difference? Is this going to make the thing more difficult?

Absolutely not! It hasn't hurt one of our men. Oh, maybe we drink a bottle more per week or month than we ever did, but even a lot of our men do not sell when they don't feel like selling, and if they've sold enough they say, "Well, that's enough for this year, I'll sell next year." When they do get a little sum of money it goes into a better studio, more paint, maybe a new suit of clothes, maybe a party for other artists. A few of us have cars. I still stick with a truck which I've always had. A lot of the artists have no cars. But it certainly goes into more paint and bigger canvases. Five different men that I know have made a little better livelihood recently, have been more successful, and they have gotten out of a cold-water flat and gone into a nice big, long studio. Some of them are painting pictures twenty-six feet long, ten feet high. Well, that's a wonderful point of liberation. If they had any mercenary reasons for such a thing, they would lose it there because they never in the world can sell a picture twenty-six feet long and ten feet high. It doesn't fit any place; it has absolutely no functional need any place. But it's their desire to do it and it's a statement of freedom against having painted little pictures for so long in a little studio with canvas that was small, and it's a statement of liberty.

The Secret Letter *Thomas B. Hess*

The following interview by Thomas B. Hess, Editor of Art News, *was held in June, 1964. It was published in the catalogue of the Marlborough-Gerson Gallery exhibition of David Smith's work in October.*

Thomas B. Hess: *You've used "found objects," tools and other things picked up around the countryside—plowpoints and old trace chains—in your sculptures.*

David Smith: Of course. The sculptures I made in 1933 were all found objects.

What's the idea behind the found object as far as you're concerned? For the Surrealists, it made a metaphysical jump between the reality of the object and the idea of a work of art.

Tom, I don't know what A Work of Art is. It changes in my life and it changes in my regard. I have no respect for it particularly.

First of all, these things have a basic geometric form that's already "found." In a recent work I made one wheel, and the other three wheels I bought by ordering them from Bethlehem Steel Co. They weigh 275 pounds apiece. They are blank forgings made by Bethlehem for 100-ton overhead trolleys. You might say they are "found" objects. I found them in a catalogue and chose them because they fitted a particular need. Are triangles, circles, and spheres "found"? They have always been there. Painters don't "come upon" subjects for a still life; the Impressionists didn't come upon their subjects. They found their trees; they chose their apples; those are all "found objects"—flowers, fruit, everything.

I find many things, but I only choose certain ones that fit a niche in my mind, fit into a relationship I need, and that relationship is somewhat of a geometric nature. They aren't meant to relate to the art. But there is a certain romantic relationship in my mind to the old handmade objects that have ceased to function.

Actually you've always chosen things that once were useful, old discarded implements; never useless things.

I don't know what useless things are.

Well, there's a lot of ornamental stamped iron in the scrap heaps.

I couldn't use what was ornament.

I mean everything I've seen you use has either been a discarded tool or a functional object which has passed its period of usefulness. But it retains a kind of beauty in terms of its lost function—like a bone.

Lots of bones. Sure.

Then there is a geometry of nostalgia?

I don't know; I don't like that word. Maybe I'm not beyond nostalgia or sentiment or any of the lower things, but Tom, don't forget, when one chooses a couple of old iron rings from a hub of a wagon, they are circles, they are suns; they all have the same radius; they all perform the same Euclidean relationship. They also have the romance of past function and new use. They have sentiment and they also have the geometry. There is no simple answer . . .

You think nostalgia implies sentimentality?

Of course; I'm full of it. I was born a Calvinist. Do you think a Calvinist ever comes on without being sentimental?

By nostalgia, I mean when you pick up the casting of the thorax of an old discarded piano and put it in your work, you always respect its integrity as a thing. As against Marcel Duchamp, for example, who mocked his urinal or hat rack. You look at your found objects with respect.

Well, let's remember my heritage. When I was a kid, I had a pretty profound regard for railroads. I used to sit down on the edge of town and watch trains go through. I used to hop trains, ride on the tops of boxcars. We used to play on trains and around factories. I played there just like I played in nature, on hills and creeks. I remember when I first sat in my father's lap and steered a car. In fact, I've always had a high regard for machinery. It's never been an alien element; it's been in my nature.

The main image in American folk poetry is the railroad; it comes and takes people away from the small town; its noises . . .

And don't forget I've worked in locomotive plants. I've sat on those goddamned engines, welding them up, hoping I could someday make sculptures as big. And I will someday. I think.

And there's the surface of some of your sculpture—oxidized iron, rust.

I kind of like rust.

The nostalgia of rust . . .

Well, it's memory.

David Smith

What was your father?

He was the manager of a telephone company—independent telephone. I was born into that. Some of the first things I played with were telephones. I took them apart and used the magnets. My father was an inventor and he invented electric things—coinboxes that you couldn't fill with slugs and things like that. He invented an electric victrola before they were ever on the market.

When I was a kid, everyone in town was an inventor. There must have been fifteen makes of automobiles in Decatur, Indiana; two blocks from where I lived there were guys building automobiles in an old barn. Invention was the fertile thing then . . . I remember airplanes flying over Decatur when I was a kid. There was a plane that's now in the Smithsonian called the Vin Fizz. Vin Fizz was a grape drink they advertised with the plane flying over town.

The danger with the American-type inventor, though, is of becoming a hick, provincial, Edison.

But one of the ideas an artist has, even though he is sophisticated and knows the whole history of art, is a kind of gnawing sense of innocence. He has to work with everything he's got. He has to focus everything, all his energies, in one direction, with the innocence that art never existed before he existed.

With an innocence that presumes a tremendous amount of sophistication and insight?

It's also arrogance. You know you don't have the innocence of a child. But with your age and culture and history, you also have that attitude. I grant each artist the right to believe that he is the only artist in the world, and the greatest.

You have to assume that every artist is also a highly cultured man. You're interested in German sixteenth- and seventeenth-century medallists and . . .

. . . in Greek and Sumerian seals and in Cubism, the Baroque and . . .

And you want a library of art books.

Sure. I love to read art books. I want to know everything that has ever been known by any man.

So you are not in the least provincial about art.

No artist I know is provincial . . .

What is your place in avant-garde art? I think you did have an idea about it in the 1930's and 1940's. I don't know if you still do. But there was a certain air of enthusiasm?

Well, I think that's true, Tom. We had no group identity in the 1930's. In the 1940's it developed when Pollock and Motherwell and Rothko were showing and seemed to become a kind of group for us, which we didn't have in the 1930's. Then it was just Stuart [Davis] and Gorky and Bill [de Kooning] and Edgar Levy and a few others. We were all individuals, sort of expatriates in the United States and in New York. The dominant style was social realism and we were always voted down. You rarely saw our work in shows, but we marched in May Day parades and we supported all the humane causes; we were all on the Loyalists' side in Spain. It was only in the 1940's, when Motherwell and those men started to develop, that there seemed to be a group of abstract artists.

The avant-garde idea, which seemed exhilarating then, now seems pretty repulsive. Of course, in those days, no one was in it for a buck.

The chance then wasn't a sale; the chance was only the privilege to exhibit. That was the point of attainment. Nobody I knew in the 1930's and 1940's made a living from sales. Artists showed their work to other artists . . .

"Totem" is a recurring word in your titles. Do you have an idea about tribal sculpture—as against folklore?

A totem is a "yes." And a taboo is a "no." A totem is a yes-statement of a commonly recurring denominator.

You mean I could ask, "Mr. Smith, are you making ritual objects for a new religion?"

No. I don't believe in anybody's religion. The bug is all those social implications in your words. I mean, everything considered, primitive society has totems and taboos, and there are totems and taboos in our society—your behavior at a Museum of Modern Art opening, or your behavior at dinner.

In your sculpture, do you have an idea of a content which concerns basic social relationships—between the work of art and the spectator, perhaps? Let's assume that the artist today works for other artists and a few friends. But is there a possibility of working for a huge imaginary audience? Could your sculpture be totems for an ideal society?

Romantically, I wish it could. But I don't see its being accepted in present capitalist society, nor in a contemporary socialist society. The only rewards that I get in the way of compliments are from other artists.

But you do enormous sculptures, many of them too big to be exhibited—except in your own backyard.

That's part of my work. I'm going to make them so big that they can't even be moved.

A lot of American artists work like that. Adolph Gottlieb was telling me that he's doing fourteen-foot-high paintings, and his gallery has ten-foot ceilings . . .

David Smith

It's a defiant position. If you can make a living selling your work, you are not going to bow to the sales angle. You are going to make things of your own nature. I would say that Adolph has a natural, built-in desire to paint them big. I know Adolph; the only times we ever showed someplace in the 1930's, we had to be able to carry our work on the subway; deliver it ourselves and pick it up. And we were just showing. We weren't selling.

Actually, you don't work for other artists; you work for yourself.

That's true, but your audience is other artists. There are always a few (very few) critics.

But isn't your work unique in that it seems to consider a wide, even if nonexistent, social role?

I think I'm an idealist.

What's the ideal? Are your totems for . . .

. . . a true socialist society, but I don't know any ideology that meets my theoretical ideal. That goes for religions or any social ideals. In other words, there is nobody I belong to or belong with.

There was a certain social setup when you were a kid in Indiana, and you had certain ideas about machinery and materials. And on your farm you've set up those huge "useless" sculptures which, to me, have a certain symbolic effect—like a book in a secret language.

The secret language, Tom, is very simple: I'm building the biggest, the best goddamned sculptures I can make within my present limits, conceptually and financially. If I could have built sculpture within my conception several years ago, they would have been twenty-five to thirty feet high . . .

The greatest part of American art in the 1930's and 1940's and even the 1950's was never built because the artists didn't have enough money to make them bigger and greater. That's where the best part of American art lies, because of our financial inability to buy what it took just to make it. Maybe it's the same for young artists today. Maybe the same for all artists, of all times.

I don't believe in the concept of anything. I believe in the conviction of the artist. The artist's conviction shows. The strength of a work is more dependent on the conviction of the artist than on a concept.

Do you remember the article Elaine de Kooning wrote about one of your sculptures in Art News *in 1951? I think the sculpture was called* The Cathedral.

That's right, *The Cathedral.*

I remember she described one form as an altar-shape and on that was a figure-shape which was pierced by a prong coming down . . .

. . . an ecclesiastical prong.

. . . and you added some molten silver to the figure and she quoted you as saying that the silver represented Purity. No one could possibly see this detail without help, or read it from the title.

Yes. Every once in a while, when I make a big rusty iron thing, I bore a hole in it and add some gold; just for the hell of it. I don't think anybody ever sees it. That tickles me a little.

The details in your work are important and you invest them with all sorts of possible meanings, private meanings, which are thrown away . . .

It's public when I show it and private when I make it. All good art that I know about is pretty private when it's made. I look for private meanings in Renaissance artists. I look for private meanings first.

Do you still work over details like that?

In some sculptures, yes; and some, no. Some sculptures are to be seen five hundred feet away and some are small and intimate, and have very intimate details.

Take last night. When I went to sleep, I was making a sculpture. I woke up twice and made drawings. I woke up this morning thinking it, you know, and I presume I was able to keep on working asleep. Sometimes I work with details and sometimes with broad statements. I don't have any conviction about one over the other.

Well, the silver you added to represent Purity, no one is going to see it unless you tell them.

I don't think it's necessary to tell anybody.

Yes, but do you do it?

The knowledge, the perception, of vision is so far greater than any statements using words, that nothing an artist can do passes beyond the vision of the beholder.

The silver would.

Do you know [in James Joyce] the Little Red Hen that scratched up a letter? Well, I'm always scratching up letters and that's one of the nice things about Joyce. There's a part of Joyce in me all my life. I read "Work in Progress" in *Transition*. It's a kind of opening, like when I first saw Cubism or Constructivism or De Stijl or any of the things I saw that I didn't know about. I love things I see and don't know about. I don't understand why other people don't like things they don't know about. It always astounds me that I can make something that somebody doesn't understand. I see everything in writing that other people write. I listen and I understand everything in music; I mean I like John Cage and Morty Feldman and Varèse and Stravinsky . . .

Did I tell you I just made 130 or 140 paintings this year from models, all nude models. I don't use drapery. When there's pussy, I put pussy in. And when there's a crack—on some of these girls who are so young you can't even see a definition—I put it in because I think it will be there, sooner or later.

You're just a stylist.

I'm a sensualist . . . but I don't use a sketch when I make sculpture, ordinarily.

You make chalk drawings on the floor.

Oh, that's when I'm in trouble.

What do you mean, "no sketches"? You're always drawing.

Well, I don't make drawings seldom. I do what I need to do, Tom, and sometimes I think I'm stronger and there are more possibilities open for invention if I don't use the sketch. I draw a lot to increase my mind or my vision, but when I work, I try to let the work make its own vision—while I keep a history of knowing behind it.

That's the most sophisticated kind of sketching . . . You also correct endlessly as you work.

I often correct pieces, and throw bad pieces away.

So whatever spontaneity you use has been filtered through the most rigorous intellectual discipline. The working process is one of constant scrutiny.

Scrutiny? I live it. I live it, and the pieces that are problems, I look at and think about three or four times a day while I'm working on other ones.

What about that spontaneity?

I use every method or approach that I need. Sometimes it is spontaneous and sometimes studied, thought, and takes a long time. Some sculptures take a couple of years before they get realized.

The point being that you stay constantly aware, an intellectual artist. You bring everything to bear on the work and that's how the art comes out.

It comes out different most of the time.

Because you can't oversee everything. The work evades scrutiny?

There is a kind of vision, usually, which is a meditated vision—as against premeditated. But I would rather call it a continuation. And then sometimes I need the contradiction to the kind of work I'm doing. Sometimes I work in what people call lines or drawing. Sometimes I need big strong cubic shapes. Sometimes I need total disrespect for the material and paint it as if it were a building . . .

Should materials be respected? Do you think "pure" is "good"?

Pretty good. It depends on the conviction of who is doing it. In relation to Ad Reinhardt's painting, pure is good.

You add color.

I'm still working on that. I've made two sculptures in tune properly between color and shape. But I've been painting sculpture all my life.

As a matter of fact, the reason I became a sculptor is that I was first a painter.

Why do you always choose bright colors?

Because they are more difficult.

Wouldn't it be easier to start with grays?

Yes, it would be easier to state color in a gentle monochrome manner, except it doesn't speak to me as strongly. I could work whites and blacks, but I think I'd have to work twenty years before I can paint circles in bright colors that succeed, and the minute I'd succeed, I would be done; that would be ended. When you get a unity, it's got to end something.

I don't see the point of whole bunches of artists today trying to do polychrome sculpture.

Now that's a dirty word, "polychrome." What's the difference between sculpture using color and painting using color?

The painters seem able to and the sculptors don't.

All right, then we haven't found it. When we find it, it's . . .

Twice . . .

. . . double. Painting and sculpture both; beats either one.

You think painting is the dominant mode?

I think reaction and response of the public and the historians are built on painting.

That's been true since the seventeenth century.

Tom, sculpture has been a whore for many ages. It had to be a commissioned thing. Sculpture was not sculpture until it was cast in bronze. Before it was cast, the man who paid for it had certain reservations and designations as to subject matter.

But modern sculpture comes out of painting like a flower comes out of the ground.

We come out of Cubism.

And Picasso and Matisse . . .

. . . are some of the people who made their greatest inventions through concepts of sculpture. And also they begin sculpture as an entity . . .

. . . as an absolute?

. . . absolute from the artist. But the reproductive processes involve something else. Sculpture is lightly considered because you see the same goddamned sculptures. They become common and that reduces the interest. The world is full of reproductions of sculpture and that is one of the defiling things about it.

I don't think that's very important. If it's good, it's good. If not . . .

It's only good when it comes from the hand and from the eye of the artist. Otherwise it's reproduction.

What about the beautiful bronze casts by Jimmy Rosati?

That's different. I'm talking about museums and dealers who make casts.

Have you ever felt in peril?

Oh, I have so many ideas; I'm not dry. I'm living ten years beyond my time . . .

I mean physically.

Physically, I'm scared something is going to happen, that I'm not going to have enough to eat. Once you've lived through a Depression, Thomas, I don't think you can outgrow it.

But your father had money and you were raised . . .

My father was a working man . . .

. . . raised with enough food.

I was raised with enough food, but I came from pioneer people. Grandmothers and grandfathers, great-grandmother, my great-great-grandmother, all of those people I talked with were early settlers. They had been deprived of salt, flour, sugar, and staples like that for periods of time. I came directly from pioneer people who were scared for survival and this reinforced my consciousness of the Depression.

To you, waste is a sin?

Right! I don't like to throw away bread . . .

You told me once that your Protestant background was a disadvantage.

It's a hell of a background, but you've got to make it with what you've got. There are no rights and wrongs. The more you meet a challenge, the more your potential may become. The one rule is that there may be no rules!

In a sense, your sculpture as a whole is about "no rules"?

I think the minute I see a rule or a direction or a method or an introduction to success in some direction, I'm quick to leave it—or I want to leave it.

Is that an unsatisfactory state?

The idea of satisfaction is like the idea of happiness—the great American illusion.

Is that the Protestant background speaking, backing away from satisfaction?

I wish to be totally unacademic.

In a sense, you always want to fail.

That's where the greatest challenge is . . . the American Protestant idea leads to revolt. A format is made to be changed . . .

I like outdoor sculpture and the most practical thing for outdoor sculpture is stainless steel, and I made them and I polished them in such a way that on a dull day, they take on the dull blue, or the color of the sky in the late afternoon sun, the glow, golden like the rays, the colors of nature. And in a particular sense, I have used atmosphere in a reflective way on the surfaces. They are colored by the sky and surroundings, the green or blue of water. Some are down by the water and some are by the mountain. They reflect the colors. They are designed for outdoors.

Like a pond . . .

. . . reflects the sky, changes color all day long. They are not designed for modern buildings.

What about the sculptures you've entitled Primo Piano ["first floor," that is, the floor above the ground floor]?

All the action takes place on the second floor.

There is the base, then a pause, then the action?

Yes. The title was a secondary thought, but, actually, there it is. The ground floor is where the desk clerks are.

And the action goes on above eye level. What about the Wagons?

I've got three on wheels. It's a kind of iron chariot, on four wheels, with open linear elements. Each section of drawing is totally unrelated, and they don't fall together. They just sit there, broken.

So the chariot becomes a kind of field where these things exist?

A longitudinal field.

And you got the idea of . . .

Actually I bought these wheels from a guy who was making two cannons for me, cannons that shoot.

What do you want cannons for, robins?

No, I wasn't going to shoot any robins. The one cannon I have is a Revolutionary War model, and it shoots frozen orange juice cans, lemonade and that sort of stuff. I save all those cans and fill them with cement and then shoot them.

How far does it carry?

Oh you can shoot it a mile, but with three ounces of powder it will shoot 700 to 1,000 feet. I also have a bronze cannon.

One of those yacht-club signal guns?

Only bigger. One was found in Lake George, originally cast in Scotland and brought over during the French and Indian War. When they pulled up a dock, they found seven old cannons shoved underneath and one was in pretty good shape. A friend of mine had his brother make a pattern of it; I had a few hundred pounds of pig bronze lying around, so they made me a bronze cannon with bronze cannon wheels. Well, on my last Wagon, I used three of the bronze wheels that were made for cannons. So it's iron sculpture and has bronze wheels.

In the longitudinal space are "drawings"?

Big forgings. I drew a number of forgings to order, about forty-five, and sent them to Pittsburgh to be made.

In steel?

Steel, yes.

It becomes a kind of classic cart . . .

. . . so you can pull them around and set them out in the field. They are too heavy for people to handle so I put wheels on them. Of course, I've used wheels a lot. As far as I know, I got the wheel idea from Hindu temples.

Those wheels of life?

They cut them out of stone on the temples to represent the processions where they carry copies of temples down the streets on wagons. Carved stone wheels. It's a fascinating idea. I went to the Museum of Science and Industry where they have square wheels.

Do you use magic? I remember a piece, fifteen years ago, with a pedestal, steel, then a plane divided into three sections and in each section there were series of shapes and, above that, some steel drawing.

That was a letter . . . and that relates to the Little Red Hen that scratched in Joyce . . . The Little Red Hen that scratched the letter up.

A steel letter.

Yes. And the letter says, "You sent for me." Something very simple. A short cryptic message. "You sent for me." All letters say, "You sent for me," as far as I'm concerned.

And there are sculptures with "H's" and "Y's"; in fact, you've been concerned with letters.

Yes.

Greek letters.

All kinds of ungreek Greek. They look like Greek and they are Greek because "Greek" is something you don't understand. And there are no "H's" or "Y's" in the Greek alphabet.

There's a "Y" except it's a trident sign . . .

. . . my "Y's" are tridents. Jean Xceron wrote my Greek for me.

And you've done some big, linear sculptures which aren't "letters"—Australia . . .

Yes, and *Hudson River Landscape;* it was a matter of drawing.

You think of drawing in terms of writing?

I don't differentiate between writing and drawing, not since I read that part of Joyce.

There is a kind of secret message?

The little hen scratched up a secret message.

"I sent for you"?

No. "You sent for me"—that's different. That's what I think the secret letter said. Nobody knows what the letter really said.

And in your sculpture of big towers . . .

. . . just rising from the earth . . .

. . . are drawings pulled up.

Yes, and it's also a challenge in engineering to make them one hundred feet high. But sometimes mine don't perform correctly; they don't look like they are standing up.

Sometimes they almost threaten to topple.

They aren't any different from light towers, but they don't look like they'll make it. Because I make them aesthetically first. Once in a while I throw in a constructive line for strength. I try to incorporate strength into aesthetics.

The only problem left is—why color?

It is a foreign introduction, but why not?

You have steel, that beautiful material . . .

Oh balls!

Steel and bronze . . .

I color them. They are steel, so they have to be protected, so if you have to protect them with a paint coat, make it color. Sometimes you deny the structure of steel. And sometimes you make it appear with all its force in whatever shape it is. No rules . . .

David Smith

IV letters

Letter to Edgar Levy, Summer, 1935

Dear Edgar,

. . . Here is the dope. We just got folders from American Express and have almost picked—barring acts of God and misfortune—the Manhattan which sails Oct 9 for Havre. We have planned to convert everything cashable to cash and go to Europe. I'm getting a few hundred—and with some old stock which has gone up—and with Dot supplying some we think we can do it. Flo offered Dottie some $'s and what with the Project work down so low it's hardly a living wage we decided quickly to go now—this being as good as any time and before inflation sets in more and the money we have or can get might as well be spent before it's worthless. . . .

However we better keep it quiet because if something came up we couldn't go—I might have too hard a time getting my job back.

Graham is in Paris. Xceron in Washington hoping to get an abstract mural with the Federal Gov.

To close the details we will be down a week before.

Regards,
DAVID SMITH

Letter to Edgar Levy from Athens, c. December, 1935

Dear Edgar,

We aren't settled yet but we soon shall be. Greek is nice—food is cheap and we had a delicious ½ bottle of vintage blanc last night costing 15¢ in our language. Their best native wine is (1926) 46¢ full bottle—these are prices at the best restaurants, not store prices. The Greek food is excellent, but we generally eat at the International where they speak French and have as the name implies international food. That way we get French, Greek, Turk, etc. The main course dishes are 18 to 35¢—big portions. Sunday we had a whole lobster each for 30¢ with salad garnish etc. Soups are 7¢, desserts 8¢. We've seen most of the ruins and museums. Jesus what a lot of stuff—and more coming all the time—stacks of crap without the dirt removed yet—just mud caked hunks of marble resembling human forms etc. I'll venture they are not fakes—for once. I'm so damned suspicious of Paris and Roman offerings. The museums have the corner on the stuff, but before I return I'll have some with me—if there is a way I'll find it. . . .

DAVID SMITH

Letter to Lucille and Edgar Levy from Athens, c. January, 1936

It has been warm. We fill an earthenware dish with artichokes, potatoes, and the two hind legs of a baby lamb and take it to the bakery to have it cooked like all good Greeks do. Then (Sunday) we sit at the sidewalk café and I drink 5 Koniaks while Dot drinks 1 lemonade—bask in the sun and talk to a few Greeks we know—some speak French—some English. Our acquaintanceship in all the countries we've visited runs to Communists. Here it is so. Our corner fruit and vegetable man is one—the shoe shiners are also (those of our acquaintance so far). Of course we've met the archaeologists and other Americans, but they are so YMCA. . . .

Edgar would be nuts in our neighborhood because of the dozens of marble yards. All colors, all depths of translucency. Chunks—slabs—and loads of tools. Even the sinks and drainboards are chiseled out of marble. They polish it to mirror smoothness. It is easy to understand the patine on the Greek and Roman statues. The Romans got it all from the Greeks. I've been reading Pliny and Vitruvius and Theophrastus and learning their methods. I intend to take color specimens from the colored statues in the museums for micro slides etc.

The American School starts excavations in a couple of days and it will be interesting to watch the process of uncovering. They are clearing a big slum area of modern houses to get down to the Byzantine level—then thru the Roman level to the Greek. One of the arche's [archaeologists] took me through the excavated areas and showed me the maps of the various stratas. The old Byzantine church that has extremely fine piece mosaics is still standing—we visited it with the Cambridge guy. It's the Daphne murals in the "Cahiers d'Art" book with the Greek sculpture. I'd like to get a chunk of that mural before we leave.

I have been painting—all 30 × 40 (small) and 34 × 40 cm. canvases that I bought cheap in Brussels. Some good picts some bad. My concepts have been sculpture for the last year that painting caught me floating for a time. I'm getting more level now and have three or four good —fairly good ones. The National Museum is near us—and what Jesus good things they have—and one realizes what jesus rococco shit the Greeks did with colored statues too—and how the f__ing Romans grabbed it all and added to it. Most of the things show better in photo —those beautiful patines, the result of age and decay—are half of the value cleaned down to clear marble without erosion. They are quite commonplace. My affinity is still with the Cyclades and the archaic bronze and iron pieces. Everybody's is I guess. . . .

Love,
DAVID SMITH

Letter to Edgar Levy, November, 1936

Dear Edgar,

. . . I've been painting and sculpting and hunting. I've got several more sculpts done since you were here. Have four deer hides now which I'm tanning to make floor rugs with—will be warm for when we stay up all year sometime, which should be in a year or two.

Had a letter from Xceron. He and Marie were married in U.S. before they went back to France.

I had to scrape five in. snow off my skylights today before I could work—got my forge installed and a smokestack out the roof made from an ex-Glens Falls lamppost (sheet metal) looks like a Greek column. Built a' stove also so studio is comfortable even in cold weather. . . . I photographed most of my sculpture but it doesn't appear any too well in the rustic setting. I'll bring the photos down which will be in a couple weeks—then I'll have to make a trip back after we get a place —to get the sculp, etc.

DAVID SMITH

Letter to J. LeRoy Davidson of the Walker Art Center in Minneapolis, January, 1942

Dear LeRoy,

I want to thank you for the exhibition and the laudatory comment. I'm sorry the gallery didn't send the two unmounted medals, they could have been shown on dish display stands.

Since I did those, the world has changed. Munich is forgotten, and the British and Halifax are trying to sell out China (so Wash. merry-go-rounders say). I don't want anyone to think my ideology herein stated is appeasement or anti-American, it is only aimed at the bad—being pro-humanitarian in the best sense—bad elements and institutions which exist and have existed in other wars even wars of freedom. Much of my data comes from government reports, and history such as Beard's. I don't know how it was received other than the Minneapolis Daily Times (Jay Edgerton), but in case anyone gets the idea that these aid the America Firsters' ideology will you issue a statement in my behalf, summing up whatever is necessary to put me straight—namely, that these attack only the bad elements, that they are attacked on an anti-freedom basis, and that these ills I attack no humanitarian could approve [of]. In the case of Jay Edgerton, he reacted on the subject closest to his home ground, but government reports, [George] Seldes, and numerous others say the press is 90% controlled by big business to partial ends. Maybe the Minn. Daily Times is in the 10%. . . .

At the time I developed these, 1937–40, they seemed to state clearly to me their anti-fascist—anti-fascist element message strong enough that there could be no misinterpretation—I hope [no one] misinterprets them, but if they do, you put them aright. Had time permitted I would have had the gallery put in an extra foreword insert of clarification.

Millie was here this summer, and I heard about you from her. I'm glad to hear you are doing so well, I hope you are on the big road. Out there ought to be a good place to raise a family. We are raising two pigs —got to butcher soon—never did it in my life—will go according to [Agriculture Department] booklet directions. LeRoy, this hermit life has its drawbacks, I long for a week of chewing the rag with the coffeepot art forum in the village and a round with the galleries and museums. But a week of it and I'm fed up and ready to get back in the mountains.

Two respectable sales lately—Modern Museum and Valentiner of Detroit Museum (only large etching to Valentiner). Have show and lecture at Skidmore in January. All of what I have said I know that you know and understand—but in case of need you have my authority to speak for me.

Our best regards to you and Martha and my thanks again for the privilege of showing at the Walker Art Center. If Hudson Walker is out there give him my regards, and tell Mrs. Lawrence to stop in when she comes again to Saratoga.

My best,
DAVID SMITH

Letter to Robert Nathan, War Production Board, May 30, 1942

Dear Mr. Nathan:

I want to place my ability in your department. Attached are opinions which place me reasonably high in my field. My hope is that the purpose and object presented seems desirable to you.

The object is to make medallions to be awarded for extremely meritorious war production service in industry. For instance an 8- to 10-inch medallion could be awarded the factory with coin-sized stamped replicas to each worker. This can be done at very small cost. Another example could be where shipyard workers, etc., have given Sunday's work gratis for production in the war effort. This sacrifice should be rewarded.

The medallions can be made without a metal priority and without affecting war effort machinery. I can produce from 1 to 100,000 medallions of superior artistic quality. There are few modern sculptors in medallion design, there are few who are equipped to carry production through the delivery of the finished work.

If my ideas strike you as feasible, I can deliver the work with one interview to establish the mechanism. Thereafter, your written statement of medallion subject matter, its use, approval of the design and statement of the quantity would be sufficient.

The Terminal Iron Works is on the Brooklyn waterfront, on which premises my studio was located. Three years ago when I built my studio here, I made a small fireproof factory unit, and retained the name for production of my own sculpture. It is equipped for all designing, specialized types of metal working, and casting.

A point I want to make regarding the reviews: namely, that the medallions were anti-fascist. From 1937 to Pearl Harbor, very few people, especially the press, recognized the anti-fascist point of view as being parallel with democratic. Most of the press overlooked this fact. This series hit the dishonorable and destructive elements of society. Certain elements, though true, might be interpreted as conflicting with the war effort. One fact I wish to restate—that my basic conception has always been anti-fascist and pro-democratic.

My final point is that I know workmen, their vision, because between college years I worked on Studebaker's production line and later on ship repair in Brooklyn harbor. Therefore, I know what my art must be to reach them. My conception must be simple, concrete, presenting in terms of American history events and things they know and respect in relation to our present efforts.

I want to do this work because I feel that my concepts meet with the progressive ideas of the people and the government today and my skill can best be used in aiding recognition of workers and producers in the war effort.

I hope you will grant me an interview.

Sincerely yours,
DAVID SMITH

Letter to Sherman Miller, American Locomotive Works, June 1, 1942

Design Department
American Locomotive Works
Schenectady, New York

Dear Mr. Miller,

I wish to apply for a job in your design department.

I feel able to qualify for the creative part of your design department by the fact that I am a nationally known sculptor, and generally considered within the first ten of the modern American group. My qualifications for the mechanical part of designing may be attested by the fact that I have had my own shop specializing in architectural and museum work from the creative design, through the pattern stage, ofttimes casting, and to the final finishing, doing whatever machine and welding work [are] needed in the final assembly.

My experience with various metals has covered the methods of fabricating, casting, and forging with the use of finishing techniques such as metal spray, electroplating, fired vitreous enamels and oxidizing, depending upon the use, location, and specifications. I have also a working knowledge of paint technology.

In addition, I have a thorough working conception of reverse carving and designing, which is applicable to medallions, name plates, insignias, and die work.

My education since high school [in] both art school and college covers seven years, with the addition of one year's research abroad. I have worked with leading architects and designers. My work has been exhibited in most museums in the United States. I have lectured at New York University, Skidmore College, etc., and have written articles such as "Art Forms in Architecture—New Techniques Affect Both" for Architectural Record, etc. Articles on my designs may be found in various periodicals from Popular Science to Time, as well as the daily press and art magazines.

While I am a recognized artist designer of the modern school, sometimes referred to as the "streamlining school," my talent is not all visionary. I know when precision and when mechanical function dictate design, and understand the technical processes a part goes through on the production line, since I am a fair machinist and a good welder as well.

I believe my experience is applicable to your tank and locomotive work. I hope that you can grant me an interview.

Sincerely yours,
DAVID SMITH

Letter to László Moholy-Nagy, c. April 1, 1944

This letter was written in response to an offer of a teaching position at the School of Design in Chicago.

Dear Moholy,

I want to thank you for your interest, but I have decided that from now on I will do only my own work; at least as long as I am financially able.

I have just recently been classified 4F by the army. I have been two years in the locomotive works and it appears that a slack period is coming in the industry so I shall be working in my studio at Bolton Landing. I have many tons of aged wood there and have ordered marble from Vermont. My metal work will be limited but I have several years' work planned in the other materials.

I feel that the locomotive business has taken more than two years out of me. I've learned much from it, but life is short, my ideas many and I hope for the rest of my life to do only my own work. You, Moholy, as an artist will understand this I'm sure.

Again I thank you for your consideration, and had I decided to teach I'm sure I could have done my best with you and your school.

With best personal regards,
DAVID SMITH

Letter to Edgar Levy, September 1, 1945

Dear Edgar,

I just got your change of address. Christ, I hope that San Francisco stuff doesn't mean you are shipping or shipped. I had hoped that you would get out, over 35 and that sort of thing.

I have meant to write you but am still not 100% [recovered] after getting out of the hospital. Got hit by 3 cars, suppose Lou told you about it.

I agree with you on the point of aesthetics. I haven't considered it long enough to make generalities—I am bound by a personal outlook, which for me gets solved by work—which I fight to do. I have a dilatory tendency—there is so much to be read—so many women to lay—so much liquor to drink—fish to catch, etc.—but I get the most satisfaction out of my work but I got to have enough of "that there"—the more I work the more it flows (the concept). Sometimes while I'm working on one piece I get a conception for a wholly new and different one—on the last two pieces—I've quickly drawn a new one, different, but suggested in a thought process which somehow took place during the manual work on the other.

I would say that my product is always about a year's work behind my conceptions, in number. Right now I have drawings and thinkings for a year's labor.

My method may have its faults. From this flowing groove one may hit off a few not as high in quality—as if one were able to preview the result from a vantage point. Yet when I get on a pinnacle and coldly calculate or preconceive a finished piece before I actually start work—it sometimes is cool in spots. Even allowing for a few ill conceived works under this emotional long flow I talk about, the end product is better— and certainly the number of works are greater. My ego flourishes on the quantity of this stream plan—and my mind rolls better when I am deep in it. One gets subject to emotional fears in this process, like poverty forcing one to give the work up for a while—death, the years are numbered—and they certainly won't last long enough to do what I have planned. I feel I have only started—I am very conscious of my inadequacy—yet every one I do makes me stronger and better—and I can see horizons and possibilities, the same as I can look back ten years and see the limits there—or are they just changes. Anyhow my concept changes only by putting finished work behind me—and as long as it's done and made it's final—I feel valid in moving on—more so than if I just changed my concept in a mental process. Of course, who do I work for, and all of that—I have discarded that worry long ago. I've myself to live with. To

David Smith

work to the fullest extent of my ability is my satisfaction. One is a product of his influences, associations, childhood, preferences, etc. That is true—I can't worry about that, the pattern is laid. I depend upon my life outlook to be honestly social and as such, indirectly or subconsciously direct me with whatever influence it wishes to exert. My faults —I fight. If my end product doesn't please—if my crudity and uncouthness mix off key in my aesthetics to nicer peoples' concepts, then I can only say what all the black collar boys say to finish an argument— fuck-em.

I'm booked for a joint show at Buchholz and Willard Jan. 2, 1946. New work at Buchholz and ten-years retrospective at Marian's. Time flies, Edgar. It doesn't seem ten years since I came back from Europe and started up again at the Terminal Iron Works in Brooklyn. I lost two years + in the Locomotive works—the same as you are losing some years in the army. As a 4F I'm damn glad I am. I've talked to some pfharts who have returned from Germany. They are full of good German people stuff—"it isn't their fault," "they were led wrong," etc. All adds up to soft cookies. "The German women treated us the best of any place," and all that bull—of course they are jerks, but a false peace can be the result. In my show I have a false-peace spectre—and a war spectre also. I hope you will be around to see it.

I've some painted sculptures in this show. My conceptions are more complex—usually 3–4 piece unities—less monolithic than before.

I'm struggling with a painting concept of related planes—where the planes or sculpture parts are modeled by painting in a way not to nullify the shape, and not to decorate the shape, but to project—by the use of both plane and paint. It's a kind of four-dimensional painting concept— not that the third dimension is indicated by modeling, but that the third dimension projects beyond that having three dimensions given and an additional dimension indicated in the painting of the three. Not very clear to you, but I have an animal urge about it.

My very best, Edgar,
DAVID SMITH

What are your discharge chances?

Letter to Marian Willard, February 23, 1947

This letter to Marian Willard, David Smith's dealer, is followed by statements Smith provided for the catalogue of his April, 1947, exhibition at the Willard Gallery.

Dear Marian:

I am disappointed that there are only three pictures. I don't like to pull in now. My costs have increased over 20% as well. My materials are more costly than I ever used before. My price goes up accordingly, and I'm willing to gamble on the selling to keep the printing and advertising in ratio. In my opinion the catalogue cost is an investment that pays off, if not during the show, during the year. All expenditures so far have paid dividends.

I've been working on your request—what my work signifies, its meaning, controls, etc. For whatever it's worth, here it is. It is the words, notes, and thoughts which I've taken out of my workbooks and grouped under their related headings. If it's used it must be used whole. No excerpts or changes. It's not explanatory [of] the photos and not all the sculptures. But there are parts that are related or explain as fully as my use of words can. Some of the statements are related to Spectres or sculpture previously made, but mostly it represents controls I've written with my work sketch.

The statements are not necessarily related and are separated by paragraph space. They are not fancy, nor poetry but as I said, verbal working controls—and impression direction. If possible, I'd rather see them in ordinary book type. I've lost affinity for Futura type types. Don't forget to put 1947 and Copyright in.

All speeches and jury duty over—that was hard money but needed.

Will send the photos when I get them back. Sent you my own file copies, having new set made. Two 5 × 7 color are included. Show them to Art News.

> Enjoy the Virgin Islands
> I have fond memories,
> Love. . .
> DAVID SMITH

The Landscape

I have never looked at a landscape without seeing other landscapes

I have never seen a landscape without visions of things I desire
and despise

lower landscapes have crusts of heat—raw epidermis and the choke
of vines

the separate lines of salt errors—monadnocks of fungus

the balance of stone—with gestures to grow

the lost posts of manmaid boundaries—in molten shade a petrified
paperhanger who shot the duck

a landscape is a still life of Chaldean history

it has faces I do not know

its mountains are always sobbing females

it is bags of melons and prickle pears

its woods are sawed to boards

its black hills bristle with maiden fern

its stones are assyrian fragments

it flows the bogside beauty of the river Liffey

it is colored by Indiana gas green

it is steeped in veritable indian yellow

it is the place I've traveled to and never found

it is somehow veiled to vision by pious bastards and the lord of Varu
the nobleman from Gascogne

in the distance it seems threatened by the destruction of gold

Spectres Are

    The race for survival—the capital dog

    Banners of Royalty with Caesarian cannon

    Race of stygosaurs with Queen Ann collars

    The chain leg of events, a thecodonts pongee heart

    Saving select bound peanut bodies for the capital conception
of natural selection

    Feed by gruel spoon to stainless held chompers

    Rolling bobbins trailing rotten yarns

    The mothers love—the asses jaw

    Rattling swords—judas pens

    Fascist mothers with voluminous vitelline vesicles

Letters

Dead birds—limp curls—racist mudball lungfish
The burning bush and the chicken dinner

Sculpture Is

My year A.D. 4 God and father, moving forms, ice cream flower odors,
fears

5 praise from a grandmother for a mud pie lion

6 the spectre human headed bird, the soul of ani revisiting
the body

7 the found book of nude marble women hidden by a
school-teaching methodist mother

Diana of the Ephesians

Egyptian embalmers and the sepulchral barge

women who utter cries beat their breasts tear their hair

the cuneiform of Nebuchadnezzar

the fight between the monster Tiamat personification of
chaos darkness disorder evil and Marduk god of light

Assyrian cuneiform where water is the parent of all
things—where universal darkness reigns—where gods
had been forgotten

The goddess Sephet, Hapi and Neith

The bright face of Shamash illuminated by the sun and
the moon

Gilgamish wrestling the lion

Eabani tossing the bull

Isthar of Nineveh standing on a gryphon

carrying mud bricks by yoke and cord

the bald-headed harpist in Thebian tomb plucking the
strings of the goddess body

the dialectic of survival

everything I sought

everything I seek

what I will die not finding

David Smith

Sketch from a series on woman and birds, in a notebook of c. 1947.

Pages from a notebook of c. 1944–54.

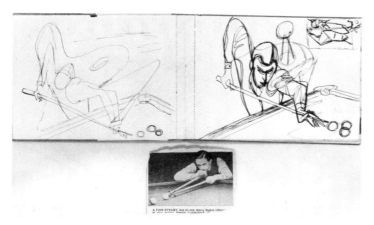

Preliminary sketches for *Billiard Player,* and clipping,
in a notebook of c. 1936.

Billiard Player (Billiard Player III), 1945. Steel,
28 x 23 x 6½ inches. Collection Roy R. Neuberger.
Photograph by David Smith.

Letter to Edgar Levy, April 24, 1948

Dear Edgar,

. . . You talk about preconceived pictures. I say sometimes yes—to a degree—and sometimes no. Sculpture is a little different. Only occasionally can I start out with no preconceived subject or point. I usually have a drawing for the start. Painting is more fluid, and you can make a lot of approaches towards a solution within or on the same canvas plane, but sculpt isn't as flexible. I haven't found a rule for myself on the approach. The end product is the thing. I get nearer each time, but that vision—can still see farther away.

. . . None of us, or very few, get the gallery we want. Yet it's still the work that arrives and not the gallery. I think the more you show the better. There is not much selling these days anyhow—so you or I cannot sell just as easy at Willard or Salpeter as [at] Rosenberg or Matisse. I would do a respectable amount of advertising however—as that is an aid, in the beginning especially.

I personally like "celebrate"—there is no better word for the meaning—and it is not our world who has misused it but the Saturday drunks who have defiled it by misuse.

DAVID SMITH

Letter to Franklin Page, June 23, 1949

In this letter to Franklin Page, of the Detroit Institute of Arts, David Smith explains his concept of the sculpture Spectre Riding the Golden Ass.

Dear Mr. Page:

The "Spectre Riding the Golden Ass" came in my Spectre series, which related to the false values and evils of our civilization. This specifically related to the noises of war and evil trumpeted through the golden mouths of asses; that which is done for money knowingly or unknowingly. It relates to the means of communication that can be purchased for gold, and the false oversincerity which gold can purchase in radio, press and movies.

Sometimes all mythology is condensed to point out present-day false values, as a dream can logically do. I am interested in the reoccurring myth, from prehistoric Egypt to the present day. I read all the cuneiform translations I can find, and I like the mythology of all cultures, the analysis of it, and the analysis of man, why he makes the reoccurring myth and justifying evil.

Of course, none of this was necessarily as conscious as that when I made the sculpture. It carries about as much in the title as I had in conscious direction. It says that a vulgar broken-winged spectre blows a trumpet through the mouth of a broken-down but golden ass, loud brass and false noises.

I don't think I can make this explanation any more exact, but I hope what I have written will help.

Sincerely,
DAVID SMITH

Letter to Jean Paul Slusser, April, 1950

In this letter to Jean Paul Slusser, of the University of Michigan Museum of Art, David Smith discusses his sculpture Tahstvaat.

Dear Mr. Slusser:

I have been thinking about "Tahstvaat" and the ideas suggested by your letter of March 31. Actually, the name was given to it by my wife, who paints under the name of Dorothy Dehner. The idea was quite abstract during its inception; and the name was one of designation, given to it before the exhibition, when we needed one for the catalogue.

I wish it to be understood as a structure. The impelling force in its making had no words nor literary statement, and the direction was intuitive. There were preliminary drawings, but at the time I was working in a fluent stream and had no statable expressions. Working alone in the country and isolated, the flow of ideas rarely takes shape in work expression.

I can remember a certain analysis related to "Tahstvaat" as being a formidable vertical structure having distinct feminine characteristics in wide open gesture, seeking protection behind the forward bone-like structure. The vertical structure is also one of a dance gesture sheltered by a solid such as a rock.

The preliminary working drawing was made in red paint and included six small sketches with a more or less final one in pen and ink. The drawing has notes relating to my procedure and to the final finish which

I had eventually intended after the piece rusted, and carried the notation . . . "red rust and grease."

The head of the vertical, and the whole of the forward protective structure is cast iron, the rest is forged fabricated steel.

This is about the limit of my recollections now, but I'll go through all my drawings for 1946 and my notebook and if I can give you more, I shall.

I am pleased that you own "Tahstvaat," and that it is in your museum. To my mind, it is one of the best I've made and I am only sorry I haven't more analysis to offer.

Most sincerely,
DAVID SMITH

Letter to Marian Willard, April 12, 1953

Dear Marian:

I agree with you; I'm also glad that Andrew did the selecting for the European show. I only wish some of the big pieces could have been included for balance. But this is the first for me in Europe outside of the outdoors Brussels show.

Saw Morris [Graves] just that one night for an hour or two. Wish he had stayed longer. I would have liked to talk to him, but it was all in group conversation. I had just arrived from Tulsa that evening after the TV show for the University. I drew pictures of apples, etc., as illustration to points on reality. My new hanging piece "Parallel 42" was suspended under lights and revolved for the cameras while the discourse was on, at least part of the time.

Had a very nice time there. A friend of the president's (art museum) took Colt and me on a salmon fishing trip up the Columbia River. We fished about 60 miles, ate and drank most of the time because no fish were biting. Lectured at Oregon University where Colt drove me, also at the museum in conjunction with Reed College. The Colts were very nice and generous with their time. I was greatly taken with Portland and the countryside. I hope someday to visit Seattle and return to Portland as well.

You haven't heard from me because of my great obligations. Got back to teach one day before vacation. Had written Jeannie to come out for vacation. When she came we talked, solved the personal difficulties and applied for an Arkansas license and were married Monday in

Eureka Springs by the Justice of Peace in a feed and grain store, with Eddie and Norma Millman as witnesses. Jeannie hadn't expected to stay but we have my apartment and only a few clothes for her but we will manage till the end of May, when we will truck back. We talked over many things and took a long chance, but it's love and will be our future, crises, offspring, hardships come what may. . . .

My drawings are going fine and fruitful (20 drawings and 4 new sculptures on exhibit at Philbrook in Tulsa, 24 drawings at Portland museum now). I'd like a drawing show next year and a sculpture show too. What do you think, do you want both or should we try to farm out the drawings, like a big drawing show—200 say—to Stable Gallery at the same time as the sculpture show? An idea to be talked over when I get back in June.

Love,
DAVID SMITH

Letter to Jean Xceron, February 7, 1956

You are a wonderful friend and thank you so much for the González information. I've already turned the article in, and have requested that a Feb. copy of "Art News" be sent you. The last two letters gave me information which I can use sometime or in answers, but I had to send the article in Jan. 1.

I suppose you've read Roberta's [González's daughter] article in the Arts [*Digest*]. She of course had family knowledge which I didn't have access to, but my article is more in examination of the work to the man and his time. I'm not a good writer, but I did as good as I could and I have no apologies. But I could have made two sculptures while I worked on it. Remember May 1935, when we walked down 57 St. after your show at Garland Gallery, how you influenced me to concentrate on sculpture? I'm of course forever glad that you did, it's more my energy, though I make two hundred color drawings a year and sometimes painting, but by having my identity as a sculptor, I can paint and I thus know myself better. But I paint or draw as a sculptor, I have no split identity as I did in 1935. Forever thanks.

I'm working hard to finish up—I'll have twenty-two standing sculptures, some big; they range in heights of 65 to 100 inches, both bronze and iron. I think this is my best so far.

I also have enough for another show this year, not so big.

I'll show about twenty drawings also in this show March 6—Come—there is no opening time or preview—Open at 10 A.M. to 6—no drinks or cookies either.

Jeannie will come for two days. I want you and Marie to meet her.

We plan to come down [for a] week or two in April when we will take you and Marie to dinner. We will have our girls with us then.

Regards and love from us all.

DAVID SMITH

Read you are in new acquisitions at the Museum.

Letter to Robert Nunnelley, June 10, 1956

Dear Bob,

I wouldn't worry about the museum job too much—maybe part-time ordinary labor would be more conducive to conceptual work—than the chi-chi of museum employment. You've got 1500, and in September rent a loft for $30/$40 month—paint—food—I'll introduce you to friends share problems—be severe in your own criticism of others in your own thinking—demand everything of yourself—live cheap and work hard—that will do more for you than anything else. 1500 should let you work the year—carefully—then look for job—or go back for summer work there and come back—there are survival jobs around—I know some, and in a year you will also. With your M.A., a part-time teaching job is possible later but the better the artist you are the better the teaching job—what you need is to see—show and associate with contemporaries, and work. Don't give it so much thought—leap—with that grubstake you can. Thinking is necessary—but when the making of works becomes the habit and identity, then the flow of work consumes the thinking element and work becomes so necessary that the thinking is a diversionary element.

I don't offer you a future in painting but for the time being, and to fill your needs—with your capital—survival can be attained in N.Y. as easily as Arkansas—with confreres and environment more stimulating.

Who knows where progression goes—it's in one's mind and in one's demand upon oneself.

Bring a bundle of work with you—it's identification and family—and keeps you related to what you have to do. It will help the new work.

I'll be in and out of N.Y. and undoubtedly my friends can help you locate with studio, etc. Don't plan to work until you have to; survey the museum jobs before you leap. . . .

Regards,
DAVID SMITH

Letter to Emanuel Navaretta, November, 1959

In the following letter, David Smith reminisces on the days of the Terminal Iron Works in Brooklyn.

Dear Emanuel,

About the ironworks—I moved in early in '34. Two Irishmen, Blackburn and Buckhorn, owned the works, a ramshackle series of buildings on the Brooklyn waterfront at the foot of Atlantic Avenue.

Blackburn was a big gentle ironmonger whose best expression was "if you can't stick your foot in it, it's flush." Buckhorn was white-collar, the job digger, and checkwriter, his was "balls and six are eight".

In '36 Blackburn sold to Buckhorn and took a job with Robbins drydock. In '39 Buckhorn sold and became a boiler inspector. Robert Henry the machinist, a friend and fellow chess-player, went to a ship repair firm in Jersey City. Buckhorn's father who had sold his Ivory Bone and Pearl Works in lower Manhattan moved in with me as the Terminal Bone and Pearl Works and I was the Terminal Iron Works. For several years we were ideal workmates each with separate quarters. Buckhorn senior was a great craftsman—he had made revolver handles for as far back as Bill Cody. We worked hard, drank our tea together, but the gaiety was gone.

The Ironworks was inside the gates of the Atlantic Avenue Ferry terminal. George Kieman who ran the "men only" saloon at 13 Atlantic Avenue had inherited it, Indians in the window and all, from his uncle Red Mike. We ate lunch, got our mail, and accepted it as a general community house. It was the social hall for blocks around. Any method or technique I needed, I could learn it from one of the habitués, and often got donated materials besides. These were the Depression days. My sculpture "Blackburn" was made afterwards in homage. One called Buckhorn I will yet do.

DAVID SMITH

Letter to the Fine Arts Committee of the Board of Trustees of Carnegie Institute, October 26, 1961

Terminal Iron Works
Bolton Landing, New York
October 26, 1961

The Fine Arts Committee of
The Board of Trustees of
Carnegie Institute
c/o Mr. Gordon B. Washburn
4400 Forbes Avenue
Pittsburgh 13, Pennsylvania
Gentlemen:

I do not wish to accept the prize your guest jury has honored me with.

I wish the money involved returned to Institute direction, and I hope applied to use for purchase.

I believe the awards system in our day is archaic.

In my opinion all costs of jury, travel, miscellaneous expenses of the award machinery could be more honorably extended to the artist by purchase.

A few years ago I was chairman of a panel in Woodstock, New York, wherein the prize system was under discussion. The majority of artists spoke against the prize system. Dr. Taylor, then President of the Metropolitan Museum, was recognized as a speaker for the prize system. He spoke eloquently and defended this as of being the donor's prerogative and ended by summing up that the prize system is longstanding and honorable and goes back to the days of Ancient Rome when a prize was given for virginity. After the applause—a hand was raised for recognition by painter Arnold Blanch. His question—would the last speaker care to qualify the technical merits for second and third prize.

Thank you and greetings.

DAVID SMITH

Preliminary sketches for *Vertical Structure,* in a notebook of c. 1946.

V writing and criticism about david smith

David Smith's Abstract Sculpture in Metals
Elizabeth McCausland

> *The earliest extended notice of David Smith's work was written by Elizabeth McCausland, art reviewer for the* Springfield Republican. *A perceptive and thorough critic, Miss McCausland interviewed Smith at some length at the Terminal Iron Works in Brooklyn and published the results in the* Republican *on March 31, 1940.*

The exhibition of abstract sculptures in steel and other metals fabricated by David Smith, now on view at the Neumann-Willard Gallery (543 Madison Avenue), is an impressive demonstration of an idea. The idea is, briefly, that modern sculpture should base itself on the technology and materials of the present instead of relying solely on methods and materials which evolved from other ages.

In taking his aesthetic and technical stand on fabrication, a method commonly used in the metal industries, David Smith puts himself in the position of denying the validity of casting. He does this not in the sense of denying other sculptors the right to employ an immemorial method, but in the sense that he as an individual has certain interests, ideas, problems, which can only be solved in relation to his own experience. His experience ranges from work in factories to formal art schools; the latter he rejects, the former he embraces as inspiration for plastic endeavor.

It is important to point out the role of freedom of thought and action in art today. Progressive artists generally are seeking ways in which their art may reach the people in great numbers. For this purpose, in sculpture, the multiple original cast by modern methods is obviously ideal. It happens that Smith is not personally interested in this objective. He would not, however, oppose it for the individual so interested. On the other hand, he would argue that he as a progressive sculptor has an equal freedom to explore and to experiment, to put to use his knowledge of the oxyacetylene torch and the tensile strengths of metals. Freedom thus means opportunity for different purposes and ideas to work together in tolerance. If one objective is right and another wrong, history will settle the point—one trusts, without blows.

Smith makes his steel sculptures in an old ironworks on the Brooklyn waterfront. If laymen still have the idea that art is an effete luxury, they should spend a morning in his "studio," where forge and other equipment stand on the cold earth. Smith meets the necessities of his environment by having the shoemaker put a half-inch layer of cork between the outer and inner soles of his work shoes.

Here he cuts steel in the shapes he needs, using an oxyacetylene torch to eat through half steel like soft wood. Then, following designs he has sketched carefully and with color indicators, he welds the pieces with his torch, thus fabricating large forms which to the eye seem as solid and monolithic as a granite boulder. It is surprising to grasp one of these abstract sculptures with a spread of four feet, and find that it can easily be lifted. The relatively light weight due to hollow construction is plainly a great boon to the sculptor, who is usually weighed down like Atlas by the bulk and weight of his work. Transportation loses its horrors.

Final touch is the applying of what may be called "organic color." Color is no new fashion in sculpture. From the Greeks on, polychrome has been a legitimate and desirable adjunct of plastic form to enhance and enrich volume. Fifteenth-century Gothic wood sculpture or twentieth-century papier-maché Gershoy fantasies, the idea is the same, and the aesthetic impact similar. But polychrome has been one material—pigment—put on another material—wood or stone.

Here Smith has made a positive aesthetic contribution. Using a different nipple and more air pressure in his oxyacetylene torch, he blows molten metal on the sculpture, as copper, stainless steel, aluminum, or zinc. A thin wire of the metal is fed through the nipple, and this melts and is forced through the air in minute particles which harden as they reach the surface. There is a sort of mechanical penetration of the basic steel, so that this color is actually "organic."

By burnishing, a brilliant patina may be achieved; the surface may be left with a kind of matte finish; metals may be mixed. Thus a variety of colors and surfaces may be obtained. For example, if a copper patina is left to oxidize, the familiar verdigris will result. Used with zinc oxide, there is a play of green against white. Another combination is to spray steel with zinc, which prevents corrosion, and then with copper. A silver and pink color is produced.

Why stainless steel on steel, someone may ask? To reduce cost is the answer. Moreover, for fabrication, industrial steel is probably better, cutting, forging, and welding more successfully.

For sculptures to be used indoors, lacquer or specially prepared waxes may be used; also the pieces can be painted, as structural steel is. They may be baked with enamels. Or may be permitted to rust. Rust is a natural color, the iron oxide ranging from yellow to purple, as in the sculpture *Interior,* which has been enhanced with bronze by brazing. Steel, left its natural color, is also beautiful; it can be polished to a high finish or left with surface irregularities, as in *Bathers,* made from an old piece of sewer pipe, where the metal was pitted from previous wear.

　　　　　　　　　David Smith

One of Smith's arguments for fabrication is that it is cheaper than casting. This seems provocative. Here is a method involving a tremendous amount of hand work and hard manual labor to produce a single piece; how is it cheaper? He points out two respects: the impossibility of casting modern sculpture except with a large number of separate casts, and the smaller cost for metal for a hollow piece. For example, a Lipchitz sculpture might require as many as a hundred casts. In assembling the individual parts, considerable damage could be done to the sculpture's original aesthetic integrity.

Steel is a material David Smith knows and loves as another sculptor loves, say, wood or stone. The purer it is the easier it cuts; cast iron or wrought iron are much harder to cut, even with the torch's piercing flame. Steel comes in a great number of thicknesses, from paper thin to half an inch. Some kinds of steels are so malleable that the sculptor can tie knots in strips. For most purposes, Smith prefers "mild" steel, which can be worked, heated, quenched, without taking a temper. It will absorb more shock and can be bent at greater angles; a hard-tempered steel will crack at a 90-degree angle. Then, the tensile strength of steel is a further advantage; great planes can be constructed which will not sag or break. Here is a plastic equivalent of the forms made possible in modern architecture by steel-frame construction.

With tools, here one comes up against the constant cry of the artist: "If only one could experiment more; test out new ideas, have proper equipment, and not have to worry about the cost of materials!" In Smith's case, the cry is particularly urgent, because he needs production-line tools to do the best possible job with his sort of sculpture. He has an oxyacetylene torch, to be sure; but the tanks of gas cost money and nipples wear out and have to be replaced. He uses a 1–3 h.p. motor to operate his burnishing buffs; but he needs more power. Many of the pieces might conceivably be "painted" with stainless steel, except for cost. And so the story goes.

For the work itself, aside from its technical interest, David Smith conceives of all kinds of uses. The three pieces reproduced [*Headscrew, Vertical Structure,* and *Structure of Arches*] indicate one use, monuments in public parks or grounds along a waterfront or seashore. *Headscrew* is plainly a marine form, while *Ad Mare,* not illustrated, employs a number of forms from ship construction. . . . it is interesting to note that these abstract designs, fabricated by the most complicated of man-made technics, fit quite simply and harmoniously into an environment of nature.

Generally Smith's sculpture is conceived of in terms which represent the modern attitude toward space. His forms are not necessarily the skeleton of the object from which he abstracts meaning, but the space which surrounds the object. Or they may be simplified expressions of the object, or sometimes, as in the cat on the hearth of *Interior,* whimsical statements. To a degree, this is a metaphysical preoccupation. Nevertheless, it is a concept which has exercised a real authority over present-day abstract artists, whether in sculpture or in painting.

A few pieces in the exhibition depart from fabrication and are cast. Here, also, Smith tries to use a modern method. *Growing Form* was cast in silicon aluminum at a foundry, a machine casting at 65 cents a pound. The sculptor was handed over crude casts, which required a great deal of his work before the final object might be considered a work of art. He had to polish and buff, to bring out the form, just as in machine castings for industrial use ultimate precision would be obtained by milling the casts.

Seen in a gallery, these sculptures speak for themselves. They are plastic, interesting, exciting. By their use of metallic color, they create an aesthetic tension between the hard, nonhuman material, steel, and the sensuous relief of the rusts, roses, silvers, dark grays, and blacks. Finally, they have been beautifully mounted by the sculptor. It is a fillip of fun that David Smith, who has no desire to work in wood, salvages lovely worn pieces of piling from the water front and uses them for pedestals.

David Smith   *W. R. Valentiner*

William R. Valentiner, a distinguished art historian and museum director, wrote this introduction to a catalogue of a David Smith exhibition held jointly by the Buchholz Gallery and the Willard Gallery in January, 1946.

One sometimes wishes that American sculpture had developed further in the direction to which early folk art pointed, instead of vying with a complex European tradition, that of an old and highly cultivated society. The masters of folk art, like those who made ship figureheads and weathervanes, had fundamental knowledge of the material they used, material such as wood and iron which could be found in their own land. When it was a question of marble or bronze sculptures, the early American artist was dependent upon imported material and the technical skill of foreign workmen. This technical ability resulted in a very un-American virtuosity, exhibited in imitations of European styles, during the classic, romantic, and impressionistic periods; sculptures were produced whose content was understandable only to a small group of intellectuals who had traveled in Europe, but who knew as little of the spiritual needs of the American masses as the sculptors who lived abroad. As a consequence of divergent influences from Italy, France, and England, the trends in sculpture ended, in the twentieth century, in an indescribable confusion, of which some of the large exhibitions of American sculpture during recent years have given striking illustration.

If sculpture was to become again a sincere expression of the time and of the character of the people, it had to start anew from the simplest beginnings. Not only a new technique, but also a new content had to be found. For no new technique has value in itself unless it expresses a profound experience of life. To imbue the new forms with spiritual elements is for that reason such a difficult task, because in our machine-loving age the discovery of new techniques has been far in advance of a spiritual development in the arts.

David Smith is one of the few American sculptors to whom the new idea is as important as the new form.

He has worked in many different materials, but most characteristic is his use of fabricated steel plates, of which he learned the qualities through work in war factories. It is the kind of material by which we are surrounded, such as in modern conveyances, equipment, and household utensils, but which has been generally used only for mechanical, not for artistic, purposes. It is not easy to adapt it to pure sculpture because two-dimensional plates have in themselves no plastic value. The forms must be cut out, the plates must be welded together in such a way that they point in different directions or shift one behind the other, thus creating the impression of space. Like all good sculpture they must be filled with vital energy producing the sensation of movement in one or in many directions. The importance of the silhouette was realized by the makers of early iron weathervanes, but these craftsmen did not unfold the pattern into three-dimensional space, since they depended upon the wind which turned the vanes in different directions like a mobile. Excellent examples of a three-dimensional conception developed from flat steel plates are the *Pillar of Sunday* and the *Cockfight,* while the expression of speed in a single direction successfully replaces the idea of static volume in such works as the *Spectre of War* or the *False Peace Spectre.*

A different three-dimensional effect is created by a group of monumental abstract sculptures meant to be placed out-of-doors. They are made of steel plates welded together into compact cubic forms with straight or curved outlines. The silhouette of these powerful compositions is usually closed, but within that framework an intense struggle of forces takes place, which holds us in suspense. As in the motors of modern machinery, the various powers are evenly balanced, curved forms interchange with straight ones, pointed with blunt ones. By walking around these sculptures, which are intended to be seen from all sides, the masses appear to be constantly shifting, revealing new views of exploding energy, of which parts seem to break through the frame unexpectedly, as if darting into space.

Again another technique is employed in those sculptures which the artist calls "classic figures." They are cast in bronze from models in wood which the artist himself cuts as separate sections. The individual forms are full and rounded, enclosing open spaces which are carefully balanced with the closed ones, and they suggest human figures in the first stage of development out of earthy forms. Sometimes the two techniques of steel plates and of bronze casts are combined, as in the *Reliquary House,* giving a variety of sharp and angular and of soft and curved forms, and providing varied surface texture.

David Smith's first success was based, to a considerable extent, upon his Medals for Dishonor, anti-war compositions of great individuality and force. In this connection it has been said of him that an artist ought not to concern himself with political problems; yet why should not the artist, with his deep insight, stress human values, especially in times when political propaganda emphasizes the opposite? Only the artist who stands in the midst of life and participates in the struggle that concerns us all can become a moral force, as in former ages when sculpture was an important influence upon the development of ethics. It is an encouraging sign that precisely the younger generation is captured by the new symbolism represented in the works of David Smith and of painters of similar tendencies, that it understands the meaning of that symbolism more easily than do those who grew up with a humanistic education. What the present generation longs for is the statement of its own problems, its own sorrows and joys, communicated in the direct manner of an understanding friend. No scholarly preparation is needed to comprehend the horrible vision *Spectre of War*—a spectre that haunts us yet— a headless monster composed of steel and weapons, rushing along with passionate fury. And affinity with the artist's feelings will certainly be evoked by the *False Peace Spectre,* a strange creature, once beautiful, but now, with torn-out feathers, fallen to ugliness.

But in most of his recent works, the artist has turned away from war obsessions. His symbolism is directed toward nature and the peaceful pursuits of men. He is absorbed with formations of growth in plants and trees, with work and pleasure in the workman's life, with folk traditions and especially with the idea of the house: The sculptor tells us of the bare structure of houses, in which outside and inside are still exchangeable, of the finished and yet open house in its relation to landscape and cosmos, of the *Reliquary House,* which is shut off from the world, and

David Smith

of the *House of the Welder* where everything is related to the owner's work—all conceptions rarely ever illustrated by sculptors, except perhaps in primitive periods when people struggled with the same fundamental problems as does the modern workman today, after two world wars.

Those who expect from art loveliness and charm instead of strength and character, those who are sensitive to sharp metal corners and rough surfaces, should keep away from David Smith's plastic works. For his art is harsh and intense and, since it is young and new, sometimes still awkward and heavy. But in its earnestness and directness, it has qualities that seem peculiarly American, such as we admire in Winslow Homer's and Marsden Hartley's paintings. At the same time, David Smith's art believes in the demands of its own epoch, in the creation of new symbols and a potent reconstruction of life. It has what de Chirico once described as the greatest need of the art of our time, "faith in ourselves, so that the revelations we receive, the conception of an image which embraces a certain thing which means 'absolutely nothing' from the logical point of view, should speak so strongly in us, evoke such agony and joy, that we are compelled to express it in art."

David Smith's New Sculpture *Clement Greenberg*

The following is Clement Greenberg's introduction to the catalogue of an exhibition of David Smith's sculpture, held at the Institute of Contemporary Art, University of Pennsylvania, Philadelphia, February 1–March 15, 1964. It was reprinted in Art International, *May, 1964.*

Short-windedness is supposed to be endemic to American artists—and writers—in this century, but of late it seems to have become just as prevalent among artists of other nationalities. The long career in which development continues throughout has become a rather rare phenomenon. David Smith's stamina as an artist is almost a unique one. By the early 1950's he had already done enough to make him the best sculptor of his generation anywhere, and had he stopped then and taken to repeating himself, his achievement would still have been enough to assure him an important place in the art of our time. But far from stopping or falling off, his art renewed itself in those years, as if to answer whatever questions about it remained. It manifested a new breadth and at the same time a new depth.

In an article in *Art in America* written in 1956, I remarked on what had used to be Smith's radical unevenness, and on how in the two or three years just preceding it had ceased being so radical. Today I would say that this unevenness has become almost entirely a thing of the past, Where, ten to fifteen years ago his misses far outnumbered his hits, in the last years his misses have become not just relatively, but absolutely rare. And he has not had to play it safer in order to make it so: he remains as adventurous as ever, and if anything, he has become even more prolific. This, too, is a phenomenon.

Smith's way of exploring and exploiting his conceptions has evolved along with almost everything else in his art. In the past he tended to overdo or overload the single piece; he would try to say too much, or say it in too much of a hurry. Now he lingers over his conceptions as they come to him, explores them more thoroughly, and—what is more surprising in the light of his past—tries to clarify what is essential in them. Smith's taste can still be bad, but somehow it no longer gets in the way very much, no longer turns what could have been successful pieces into bad ones—or into pieces that look bad at least on first sight and which have to "age" in order to reveal whatever merits they have. Now Smith seems to ride over his bad taste and make it peripheral.

Back in the late 1940's he had already begun, rather sporadically and rather hesitantly, to work out certain ideas in series of pieces that were like variations on a single theme. Significantly, the proportion of successes to failures in these series was much higher than it was in Smith's other work of that time. But only in the early 1950's did he commit himself to doing series in a regular way, and it was then, too, that each series became more extended. Where they used to run to no more than a half-dozen sculptures each, they now began, as in the Agricola and Tanktotem groups, to run to as many as two dozen or more. And as the pieces in each series multiplied, they became less abrupt as variations, more nuanced. But the nuancing, instead of making Smith's manner more involuted or ambiguous, only made it more logical and direct.

Smith has never worked in a single direction or vein within any given span of time; he has from the start practiced several manners concurrently—and sometimes they were more than several, to the confusion of the art public and the cost of his public "image." Over the last years, however, his different manners or veins separate themselves in a more consistent and distinct way. This, too, is part of his ongoing development. Three clearly demarcated veins are now distinguishable in his work: a strictly geometrical "cube-shaft-and-plate" manner in stainless steel; a less apparently geometrical "flat cut-out" manner in painted sheet metal; and a freehand, only roughly geometrical "rod-and-disc" manner in steel and iron, using both found or prefabricated and expressly forged or cast elements. All three manners go back more or less to the beginnings of Smith's maturity, but the last goes back the furthest and brings to its fullest and best fruition a cluster of ideas whose seed lies in things Smith did as long ago as the late 1930's. This last manner is the one exclusively represented in the present selection of sculptures.

These come from a group of twenty-six divided into three series called, respectively, Voltri-Bolton, Voltron, and V.B. The roman numerals by which the pieces are individually identified run continuously, however, beginning with Voltri-Bolton and ending with V.B. Because of this and because of the homogeneity of style throughout, the entire group can be considered a single unified series that can be referred to most conveniently as Voltri–Bolton Landing. Smith started the series in the fall of 1962 on his return to his home in Bolton Landing, New York, from a short but crowded stay in Italy, and he finished it (if it is finished) late this past fall. He had had a crate of massive old tongs, pincers, wrenches, and other tools shipped home with him from Voltri, and one or more of these is incorporated in every piece of the series (though nothing in it is directly related either stylistically or thematically to the monumental works he created, in one prodigious burst of energy and inspiration, while in Voltri).

The pretext—I would hardly call it the theme—of all the Voltri–Bolton Landing pieces is the upright human figure. Not so long ago it had had to compete with the bird and animal figure in Smith's imagination. Now it has become completely dominant, and not only in the "rod-and-disc" vein but also in the stainless steel one. The human figure suggests—or is suggested by—verticality, narrowness, tapering. Connotations of solidity used, however, to cling to it as they did not to the bird figure, which was a far more obvious pretext for open, calligraphic design. Now Smith has expunged every last one of these connotations from his "rod-and-disc" sculptures. If any such remain in his art, they are confined to stainless steel or, even more uncertainly, to sheet metal. The Voltri–Bolton Landing pieces are given over entirely to transparency and cursiveness.

But the cursiveness of Smith's drawing-in-air is not as cursive, not as nervous, as it once was. In the Voltri–Bolton Landing series, as elsewhere in his art, his drawing takes on more and more of geometrical regularity. It becomes more and more the kind of drawing that moves from the elbow or shoulder rather than from the wrist or fingers. And it converges with the newest developments in abstract painting, where the smears and squiggles of painterliness are ceding to cleaner, more anonymous handling. Smith's art was never notable for the excrescences, the fuzzed and irregular surfaces, and the curlicues that mark most of postwar abstract sculpture, but whatever it did show of such things has almost completely disappeared by now. As geometrical as Smith's drawing and design may become, nothing in his art associates itself with geometrical art as we know it from the past. There is no flavor in it of De Stijl or of the Bauhaus or even of Constructivism (much less of streamlined "modernism"). This is because the geometrical does not enter Smith's art by doctrinal right and impose itself as a restriction. He chooses it as but a means among other means available to him, and he prefers it simply for the sake of its directness and economy. The regularity of contour and surface, the trued and faired planes and lines, are there in order to concentrate attention on the structural and general as against the material and specific, on the diagrammatic as against the substantial; but not because there is any virtue in regularity as such.

It would not do, however, to dwell too long on the geometrical aspects of Smith's art in the present case. Contradictory impulses are at work, and the triumph of the art lies—as always—in their reconciliation. Hardly a piece in the Voltri–Bolton Landing series makes the impression of geometrical regularity as a whole. If there is geometry here, it is geometry that writhes and squirms. Only when we inspect parts or details do we notice how simplified and trued and faired everything—or almost everything—is. The relatively simple and forthright has been put together to form unities that are complex and polymorphous. Smith's drawing itself may have become less nervous, but the unities of structure which it creates remain almost as much so as before.

The absence in many cases of applied color or finish of any sort in these particular sculptures is part of the directness and part of the nervousness. The raw, discolored surfaces of the iron or steel members may be found a little repellent here and there, but by the same token they tend to efface themselves. As I have said, Smith aims at the diagrammatic as against the substantial and textured. Here the diagrammatic enters by paradoxical means. The discoloration is too natural, too casual, to make anything but a negative contribution. Polished or painted surfaces might in particular instances, if not in others, attract the eye too much, and the attracted eye lingers, while the unattracted eye hastens toward the essential. (I am not playing on words here, but reporting my own experience.) For all that, the question of color in Smith's art (as in all recent sculpture along the same lines) remains a vexed one. I don't think he has ever used applied color with real success, and the Voltri–Bolton Landing pieces benefit by his having abstained from it. . . . Felicity comes more easily to Smith than it used to. But it is still by no means an easy felicity. I am not able to talk about the content of Smith's art because I am no more able to find words for it than for the ultimate content of Quercia's or Rodin's art. But I can see that Smith's felicities are won from a wealth of content, of things to say; and this is the hardest, and most lasting, way in which they can be won. The burden of content is what keeps an artist going, and the wonderful thing about Smith is the way that burden seems to grow with his years instead of shrinking.

selected bibliography

Writings by David Smith, and Interviews

(In chronological order)

"Abstract Art." *The New York Artist,* I (April, 1940), 5–6.

"Sculpture; Art Forms in Architecture—New Techniques Affect Both." *Architectural Record,* LXXXVIII (October, 1940), 77–80.

Text for *Medals for Dishonor.* New York: Willard Gallery, November, 1940. Exhibition catalogue.

"The Landscape"; "Spectres Are"; "Sculpture Is." *David Smith.* New York: Willard Gallery, April, 1947. Exhibition catalogue.

"I Have Never Looked at a Landscape" and "Sculpture Is." *Possibilities,* I (Winter, 1947–48), 25.

"The Golden Eagle . . . A Recital" and "Robinhood's Barn." *Tiger's Eye,* I (June, 1948), 81–82.

Captions for *David Smith.* New York: Willard Gallery, March, 1951. Exhibition catalogue.

"The Language is Image." *Arts and Architecture,* LXIX (February, 1952), 20–21, 33–34. Excerpts in "Hudson River Landscape." *Bennington Magazine,* III (Spring, 1952), 16–17, and reprinted in *Bennington College Alumnae Quarterly,* III (November, 1952).

"Who Is the Artist? How Does He Act?" *Everyday Art Quarterly,* Minneapolis: Walker Art Center, No. 23 (Winter, 1952), 16–21. Reprinted in *Numero* (Florence, Italy), No. 3 (May–June, 1953), 21.

Statement in *12 Peintres et sculpteurs Américains contemporains.* Paris: Musée National d'Art Moderne, April, 1953. Exhibition catalogue.

Statement in "Symposium: Art and Religion." *Art Digest,* XXVIII (December 15, 1953), 11, 32.

"Thoughts on Sculpture." *College Art Journal,* XII (Winter, 1954), 96–100. Reprinted in *David Smith, 1906–1965.* Cambridge, Massachusetts: Fogg Art Museum, September, 1966, pp. 99–101. Exhibition catalogue.

"Second Thoughts on Sculpture." *College Art Journal,* XIII (Spring, 1954), 203–7.

"González: First Master of the Torch." *Art News,* LIV (February, 1956), 34–37, 64–65.

"Sculpture and Architecture." *Arts,* XXXI (May, 1957), 20.

Letter to the Editor. *Arts,* XXXI (June, 1957), 7. (Denying authenticity of comments attributed to Smith in Selden Rodman, *Conversations with Artists,* New York: Devin-Adair, 1957.)

Statement in "Is Today's Artist With or Against the Past?" *Art News,* LVII (September, 1958), 38, 63.

Statement in *The Museum and Its Friends—18 Living American Artists.* New York: Whitney Museum of American Art, March, 1959, pp. 36–37. Exhibition catalogue. (Excerpt from speech given on WNYC, December 30, 1952.)

"Notes on My Work." *Arts,* XXXIV (February, 1960), 44–49. Reprinted in *David Smith, 1906–1965.* Cambridge, Massachusetts: Fogg Art Museum, September, 1966, pp. 102–3. Exhibition catalogue.

Letter to the Editor. *Arts,* XXXIV (June, 1960), 5; *Art News,* LIX (Summer, 1960), 5. (Protests owner's painting of Smith's *17 h's.*)

Statement in "Sculpture Today." *The Whitney Review,* 1961–62.

"David Smith." Interview with Katherine Kuh in *The Artist's Voice: Talks with Seventeen Artists,* New York: Harper and Row, 1962, pp. 219–34. Reprinted in

David Smith 1906–1965. Cambridge, Massachusetts: Fogg Art Museum, September, 1966, pp. 104–5. Exhibition catalogue.

Facsimile of letter to David Sylvester. In Giovanni Carandente, *Voltron*, Philadelphia: Institute of Contemporary Art, University of Pennsylvania, 1964, pp. 11–15.

"David Smith Interviewed by David Sylvester." *Living Arts*, I (April, 1964), 4–13.

"The Secret Letter." Interview with Thomas B. Hess in *David Smith,* New York: Marlborough-Gerson Gallery, October, 1964. Exhibition catalogue.

"Some Late Words from David Smith." Gene Baro, editor. *Art International,* IX (October, 1965), 47–51.

David Smith by David Smith. Edited by Cleve Gray. New York: Holt, Rinehart and Winston, 1968. (Excerpts from speeches, articles, notes, and letters by David Smith.)

"Memories to Myself." *Archives of American Art Journal*, VIII (April, 1968), 11–16. (Speech given at the 18th Conference of the National Committee on Art Education, Museum of Modern Art, May 5, 1960.)

"Notes for *David Smith Makes a Sculpture.*" *Art News,* LXVIII (January, 1969), 35–38. Written in 1951 for Elaine de Kooning's article "David Smith Makes a Sculpture." *Art News,* L (September, 1951), 38–41.

Writings About David Smith

(In alphabetical order)

American Association of University Women. *David Smith*. Catalogue of a traveling exhibition, 1946–47. (8 pp.)

BANNARD, DARBY. "Cubism, Abstract Expressionism, David Smith." *Artforum,* VI (April, 1968), 22–32.

BARO, GENE. "David Smith: The Art of Wholeness." *Studio International,* CLXXII (August, 1966), 69–75.

———. "David Smith (1906–65)." *Contemporary Sculpture, Arts Yearbook,* No. 8 (1965), 100–105.

BLAKE, WILLIAM and CHRISTINA STEAD. Forewords to *Medals for Dishonor.* New York: Willard Gallery, November, 1940. Exhibition catalogue.

CARANDENTE, GIOVANNI. *Voltron.* Philadelphia: Institute of Contemporary Art, University of Pennsylvania, 1964.

CHERRY, HERMAN. "David Smith." *Numero* (Florence, Italy), No. 3 (May–June, 1953), 20.

CONE, JANE HARRISON. "David Smith." *Artforum,* V (June, 1967), 72–78.

———. Introduction to *David Smith, 1906–1965.* Cambridge, Massachusetts: Fogg Art Museum, 1966. Exhibition catalogue.

COOKE, LESTER H. "David Smith." *I 4 Soli,* No. 1 (January–February, 1955), 13–15.

"David Smith." *Notes and Comment from the Walker Art Center,* Minneapolis, VI (May, 1952), 1–2.

"David Smith." *II Documenta 1959, Skulptur.* Kassel, Germany. pp. 170–71. Exhibition catalogue.

"Feature: A Tribute to One of the Greatest Sculptors of Our Time, David Smith (1906–1965)." *Art in America,* LIV (January–February, 1966), 24–48.

FRY, EDWARD F. Introduction to *David Smith.* New York: Solomon R. Guggenheim Museum, March, 1969. Exhibition catalogue.

GEIST, SIDNEY. "A Smith as Draftsman." *Art Digest,* XXVIII (January 1, 1954), 14.

GOOSEN, EUGENE C. "David Smith." *Arts,* XXX (March, 1956), 23–27.

GREENBERG, CLEMENT. "David Smith." *Art in America,* XLIV (Winter, 1956–57), 30–33, 66.

———. "David Smith's New Sculpture." Foreword to *David Smith: Sculpture and*

Drawings. Philadelphia: Institute of Contemporary Art, University of Pennsylvania, February, 1964. Exhibition catalogue. Reprinted in *Art International,* VIII (May, 1964), 35–37.

———. Review of *American Sculpture of Our Time* exhibition at the Willard and Buchholz galleries, New York. *The Nation,* CLVI (January 23, 1943), 140–41.

———. Review of *David Smith* exhibition at the Willard and Buchholz galleries, New York. *The Nation,* CLXII (January 26, 1946), 98–110.

HUNTER, SAM. "David Smith." *Museum of Modern Art Bulletin,* XXV (1957).

———. "David Smith's New Sculpture." Foreword to *David Smith.* New York: Otto Gerson Gallery, October, 1961. Exhibition catalogue.

JACOBS, JAY. "David Smith Sculpts for Spoleto." *Art News Annual,* XXIX (1964), 42–49, 156–158.

KOONING, ELAINE DE. "David Smith Makes a Sculpture." *Art News,* L (September, 1951), 38–41, 50–51.

KOZLOFF, MAX. "David Smith at the Tate." *Artforum,* V (November, 1966), 28–30.

KRAMER, HILTON. "David Smith: Stencils for Sculpture." *Art in America,* L (Winter, 1962), 32–43.

———. "David Smith's New Work." *Arts,* XXXVIII (March, 1964), 28–35.

———. Foreword to *David Smith: A Memorial Exhibition.* Los Angeles: Los Angeles County Museum of Art, November, 1965. Exhibition catalogue.

———. "The Sculpture of David Smith." *Arts,* XXXIV (February, 1960), 22–41.

KRASNE, BELLE. "A David Smith Profile." *Art Digest,* XXVI (April 1, 1952), 12–13, 26, 29.

KRAUSS, ROSALIND. Introduction to *David Smith: Eight Early Works 1935–38.* New York: Marlborough-Gerson Gallery, April, 1967. Exhibition catalogue.

———. Introduction to *David Smith: Small Sculptures of the Mid-Forties.* New York: Marlborough-Gerson Gallery, May, 1968. Exhibition catalogue.

———. "The Essential David Smith." *Artforum,* VII (February, 1969), 43–49.

———. *Terminal Iron Works; The Sculpture of David Smith.* Cambridge, Massachusetts: The MIT Press, 1971.

McCAUSLAND, ELIZABETH. "David Smith's Abstract Sculpture in Metals." *Springfield Republican,* March 31, 1940.

McCOY, GARNETT. "The David Smith Papers." *Archives of American Art Journal,* VIII (April, 1968), 1–11.

MELTZOFF, STANLEY. "David Smith and Social Surrealism." *Magazine of Art,* XXXIX (March, 1946), 98–101.

MOTHERWELL, ROBERT. "David Smith: A Major American Sculptor." *Vogue,* CLV (February, 1965), 134–39, 190–91.

———. "For David Smith." Foreword to *David Smith.* New York: Willard Gallery, April, 1950. Exhibition catalogue.

NAVARETTA, E. A. "New Sculpture by David Smith." *Art in America,* XLVII (Winter, 1959), 96–99.

NEMEROV, HOWARD. "Four Soldiers—A Sculpture in Iron by David Smith." *David Smith.* New York: Willard and Kleeman galleries, April, 1952. Exhibition catalogue.

O'HARA, FRANK. "David Smith: The Color of Steel." *Art News,* LX (December, 1961), 32–34, 69–70.

PORTER, FAIRFIELD. "David Smith: Steel Into Sculpture." *Art News,* LVI (September, 1957), 40–43, 54–55.

RILEY, MAUDE. "David Smith, Courtesy American Locomotive." *Art Digest,* XVII (April 15, 1943), 13.

RODMAN, SELDEN. *Conversations with Artists.* New York, Devin-Adair, 1957, pp. 126–30.

ROSATI, JAMES. "David Smith (1906–65)." *Art News,* LXV (September, 1965), 28–29.

RUBIN, WILLIAM. "David Smith." *Art International,* VII (December, 1963), 48–49.

VALENTINER, WILLIAM R. Foreword to *David Smith.* New York: Willard and Buchholz galleries, January, 1946. Exhibition catalogue.

———. "Sculpture by David Smith." *Arts and Architecture,* LXV (August, 1948), 22–23, 52.

WATSON, ERNEST. "David Smith." *American Artist,* IV (March, 1940), 20–22.

index

Index